Fast Favorites from McCall's Quilting

Martingale®
& C O M P A N Y

Fast Favorites from *McCall's Quilting*
© 2010 by *McCall's Quilting*

That Patchwork Place® is an imprint of
Martingale & Company®.

Martingale & Company
19021 120th Ave. NE, Ste 102
Bothell, WA 98011-9511 USA
www.martingale-pub.com

Credits

President & CEO: Tom Wierzbicki

Editor in Chief: Mary V. Green

Managing Editor: Tina Cook

Developmental Editor: Karen Costello Soltys

Copy Editor: Sheila Chapman Ryan

Design Director: Stan Green

Production Manager: Regina Girard

Illustrator: Laurel Strand

Text & Cover Designer: Stan Green

Photographers: Mellisa Mahoney & Brent Kane

Photo Stylist: Ashley Slupe

McCall's Quilting, ISSN 1072-8395, is published bimonthly by Creative Crafts Group, LLC, 741 Corporate Circle, Suite A, Golden, CO, 80401, www.mccallsquilting.com.

Printed in China
15 14 13 12 11 10   8 7 6 5 4 3 2 1

Library of Congress Cataloging-in-Publication Data is available upon request.

ISBN: 978-1-60468-026-3

Mission Statement
Dedicated to providing quality products and service to inspire creativity.

Contents

Introduction

Many adjectives have been used to describe the quilts featured on the pages of the *McCall's Quilting* family of magazines: beautiful…traditional…trendy… challenging…sophisticated. We pride ourselves on publishing accurate, complete patterns for quilts of *all* these descriptions. But *fast*? Yes, fast quilts, too! In today's world, quilters are busier than ever before, and patterns for truly fast quilts are much in demand.

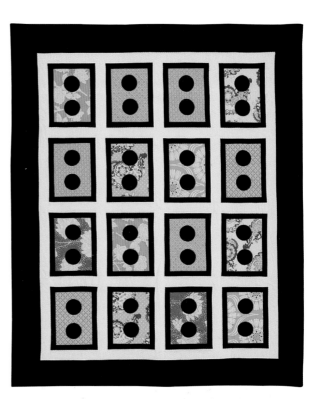

When we're looking for fast quilts to present to our readers, we search for designs that stitch up quickly, yet are creative and original as well. Anyone can design a fast quilt that looks fast. But to design a fast quilt that looks classic or artistic, exciting or lovely, fun or even complex—that takes real talent. We think you'll agree that the quilts in this book are proof that our contributing designers have that talent, and more to spare.

A number of these quilts were made using precut fabric packs, a great way to speed construction. Whether you're using fat quarters, Jelly Roll strips, fat eighths, or one of the other precuts now on the market, smaller fabric pieces are easy to handle and subcut, and allow a large variety of prints to be used in a single project. Quilters love scrappy quilts for their warmth, depth, and interest, and using precut fabrics is a perfect way to achieve this look quickly.

You'll also find a number of time-saving sewing techniques in these patterns. Strip piecing, machine appliqué, even a sure-fire method for piecing circles... each will help you make the most of your precious sewing minutes. When you get more accomplished in a shorter period, you have time left over to make more quilts!

And finally, because we know quilts are not one-size- or one-color-suits-all, several of these patterns include size or color options. Most are easily adaptable to many different sizes and color schemes, but we've taken the work out of that for you for a few patterns, to save *more* time and start you on your way to a fast, easy custom quilt design.

There's never enough time for all the quilting we dream of doing, but there's nearly always enough time to make one of the fast, unique quilts patterned in these pages. And there's no time like the present to start!

Beth Hayes
Editor in Chief
McCall's Quilting

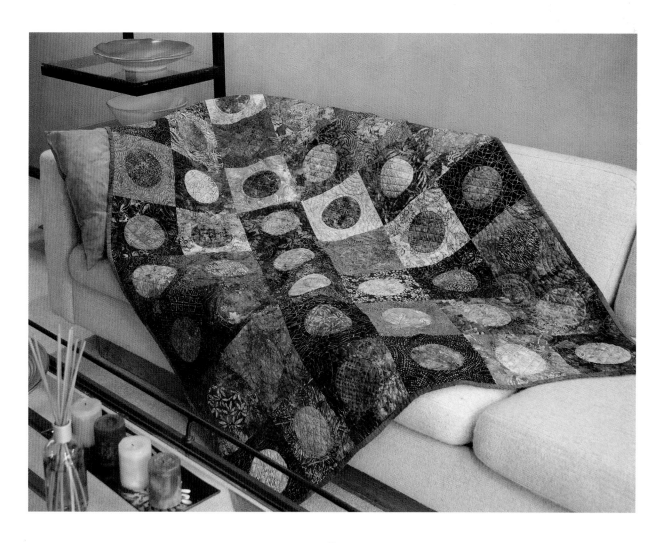

Two-Scoop Sundae

HAVE YOU BROUGHT HOME ANY LUSCIOUS FAT-QUARTER PACKS LATELY? If so, then this design is just the one you've been looking for. Note that Lisa substituted a few blue polka-dot squares for the assorted blue-and-green squares. You will have sufficient yardage to do likewise if you wish. When the quilt center is assembled, a secondary pattern similar to a Shoofly block emerges. What a sweet treat!

Finished quilt size: 81½" x 92"
Number of blocks and finished size:
30 pieced blocks, 9" x 9"

Fabric Requirements

- White-on-white print (blocks, sashing, middle border), 4⅛ yards

- Assorted yellow-green-and-white prints and striped fabrics (block centers, pieced binding), 10 fat quarters* *total*

- Blue polka-dot fabric (sashing posts, inner border), ¾ yard

- Assorted blue-and-green prints (blocks, pieced binding), 12 fat quarters* *total*

- Green large-scale print (outer border), 2½ yards

- Backing (piece widthwise), 7⅝ yards

- Batting, Queen size

A fat quarter is an 18" x 20" to 22" cut of fabric.

Cutting Instructions

White-on-white print:
*4 strips, 2" x 80", pieced from 8 strips, 42" long
20 strips, 2" x 20"
131 strips, 2" x 9½"
22 rectangles, 5" x 9½"
4 squares, 5" x 5"
26 strips, 2" x 5"

Assorted yellow-green-and-white prints and striped fabrics—cut from *each*:
1 strip, 6½" x 20" (10 total)
1 strip, 2½" x 20" to 22" (for binding; 10 total)

Blue polka-dot fabric:
*4 strips, 2" x 78", pieced from 8 strips, 42" long
42 squares, 2" x 2"

Assorted blue-and-green prints—cut from *each*:
*1 strip, 2½" x 20" to 22" (for binding; 12 total)
14 squares, 4" x 4" (168 total)

Green large-scale print:
4 strips, 6½" x 86", cut on lengthwise grain

Cut first.

Piecing the Blocks and Units

❶ Sew the white 20" strips to the sides of the assorted yellow-green-and-white 6½" strips. Make 10 total. Press in the direction of the arrows and cut into 30 segments, 6½" wide.

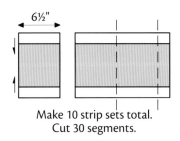

Make 10 strip sets total.
Cut 30 segments.

Lisa Christensen designed this fat-quarter friendly bed quilt.
Machine quilted by Valerie Sneed of The Olde Green Cupboard.

❷ Stitch white 2" x 9½" strips to the sides of a 6½" segment from step 1 to make the block center. Make 30 total.

Make 30 total.

❸ Draw a diagonal line on the wrong side of an assorted blue-and-green 4" square. Place the marked square on the corner of a block center from step 2, right sides together and raw edges aligned. Stitch on the drawn line; trim away and discard the excess fabric. Press open. Repeat on the remaining corners to make a block. Make 30 total.

Make 30 total.

❹ In the same manner, use two assorted blue-and-green 4" squares and the white 5" x 9½" rectangles to make edge units. Make 22 total. Use the remaining blue-and-green 4" squares and the white 5" squares to make corner units. Make four total.

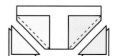

Make 22 total.

Make 4 total.

Quilt-Top Assembly

Refer to the assembly diagram for the following steps.

❶ Watching orientation, stitch the top and bottom rows using two corner units, six white 2" x 5" strips, and five edge units each. Stitch seven sashing rows using two white 2" x 5" strips, six blue polka-dot 2" squares, and five white 2" x 9½" strips each. Stitch six block rows using two edge units, six white 2" x 9½" strips, and five blocks each. Sew all the rows together as shown.

❷ Stitch a blue polka-dot strip to each side of the quilt top; trim even with the top and bottom. Sew the remaining blue polka-dot strips to the top and bottom; trim even with the sides. Sew a white 80"-long strip to each side; trim even. Sew the remaining white strips to the top and bottom; trim even. Stitch a green print 86"-long strip to each side; trim even. Stitch the remaining green strips to the top and bottom; trim even.

Quilting and Finishing

❶ Layer, baste, and quilt. Valerie machine quilted an allover flower and leaf design.

❷ To make the pieced binding, sew the 2½" x 20" to 22" strips together as shown, alternating colors. Bind the quilt with the pieced strip.

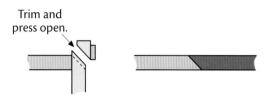

Trim and press open.

Assembly diagram

Star-Spangled Banner

WHAT A GREAT SCRAP QUILT! Feel free to repeat some of the fabrics—Ellie repeated a few of the reds. Select fabrics with different prints and textures. When making the blue strip sets, use blues with contrasting values.

Finished banner size: 16¾" x 31¾"

Fabric Requirements

- Assorted red prints, ½ yard *total*
- Assorted ivory prints, ½ yard *total*
- Assorted blue prints, ½ yard *total*
- Navy print (binding), ⅜ yard
- Backing, ¾ yard
- Batting size, 24" x 40" piece
- Paper-backed fusible web, ½ yard

Cutting Instructions

The star pattern, printed without a seam allowance for paper-backed fusible web, is on page 12.

Assorted red prints—cut 18 *matching sets* **of:**
*1 strip, 1¾" x 12"
1 square, 1¾" x 1¾"

Assorted ivory prints—cut a *total* **of:**
*18 strips, 1¾" x 12"
15 using pattern A (see "Adding the Stars" on page 12)

Assorted blue prints:
Cut 7 matching sets of:
   *1 strip, 1¾" x 12"
   1 square, 1¾" x 1¾"
Cut a total of:
   7 strips, 1¾" x 12"

Navy Print:
3 strips, 2½" x 42"

Cut first.

Piecing the Banner Top

❶ Sew the assorted red and ivory 1¾" x 12" strips together as shown. Make 18 total. Press in the direction of the arrow. From each strip set cut six segments, 1¾" wide, for 108 total.

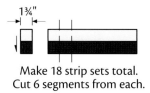

Make 18 strip sets total.
Cut 6 segments from each.

❷ Stitch together six matching segments and a matching red 1¾" square to make a red/ivory row. Make 18 total.

Make 18 total.

❸ In the same manner, use the assorted blue print 1¾" x 12" strips to make seven strip sets as shown. Press; cut 42 segments.

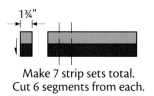

Make 7 strip sets total.
Cut 6 segments from each.

❹ Stitch seven blue rows using six matching segments and one matching blue 1¾" square each.

Make 7 total.

Ellie Brown designed this banner that's perfect to display during all the patriotic holidays.
Machine quilted by J. Renée Howell.

❺ Referring to the assembly diagram, arrange and stitch the blue rows and red/ivory rows together.

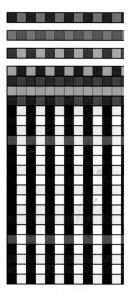

Assembly diagram

Adding the Stars

❶ Trace 15 of pattern A on the paper side of paper-backed fusible web. Cut apart, leaving a small margin beyond the drawn lines. Following the manufacturer's instructions, fuse to the wrong side of the appropriate fabric; cut out on the drawn line.

❷ Using the seams as a placement guide as shown, position the stars. Following the manufacturer's instructions, fuse in place.

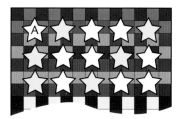

❸ Using a blanket stitch, appliqué the edges by hand or machine.

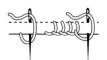

Blanket stitch

Quilting and Finishing

Layer, baste, and quilt. The featured banner was machine quilted in the ditch. Bind with navy print.

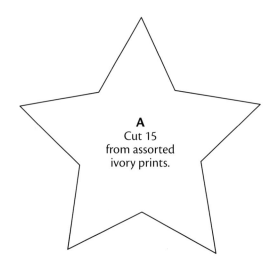

A
Cut 15
from assorted
ivory prints.

Cottage Kitchen

THIS WARM COUNTRY CHARMER owes much of its distinctive look to the liberal use of plaid fabrics—and the sashing arrangement subtly echoes the plaid theme on a larger scale. An easy pieced border creates additional interest, and bias-cut plaid binding provides the perfect finishing touch.

Debbie fussy-cut the fabric for the appliquéd flower centers to feature the bold lines of the red plaid. Be careful to use an accurate ¼" seam allowance during construction so the pieced outer border strips fit well.

Finished quilt size: 44½" x 44½"
Number of blocks and finished size:
9 Propeller blocks, 10" x 10"

Fabric Requirements

- Tan print (blocks, four-patch border squares), ⅝ yard

- Red plaid (blocks, outer border, appliqué, bias-cut binding), 1⅝ yards

- Green plaid (blocks, four-patch border squares, appliqué), ⅝ yard

- Red print (blocks, sashing posts, inner border, appliqué), ⅝ yard

- Light gold plaid (blocks, sashing), ½ yard

- Dark gold print (appliqué), ¼ yard

- Backing, 3 yards

- Batting, Twin size

This mad-for-plaid quilt was designed by Debbie Wiesner.

Cutting Instructions

Appliqué patterns, printed without a seam allowance for paper-backed fusible web, are on page 17.

Tan print:
*1 strip, 2½" x 42"
18 squares, 4⅞" x 4⅞"

Red plaid:
*2 strips, 4½" x 28½"
*2 strips, 4½" x 32½"
*1 bias-cut strip, 2½" x 188", cut from a 24" square**
18 squares, 4⅞" x 4⅞"
4 squares, 4½" x 4½"
6 using small flower-center pattern

Green plaid:
4 strips, 2½" x 42"
12 using leaf pattern

Red print:
*3 strips, 2½" x 42"
*4 strips, 1½" x 42"
4 squares, 2½" x 2½"
6 using large flower-center pattern

Light gold plaid:
9 squares, 2½" x 2½"
12 strips, 2½" x 10½"

Dark gold print:
6 using flower-petal pattern

*Cut first.
**Instructions for how to make continuous bias from a square are on page 95.*

Piecing the Blocks and Four-Patch Squares

❶ Draw a diagonal line on the wrong side of a tan print 4⅞" square. Place the marked square on a red plaid 4⅞" square, right sides together. Sew ¼" on each side of the marked line; cut apart on the marked line. Press open to make pieced squares. Use 18 squares to make 36 units.

Make 36.

❷ Sew green and red 2½" x 42" strips together. Make three. Press in the direction of the arrow. Cut into 36 segments, 2½" wide. In the same manner, sew a tan and green strip together and cut into 12 segments, 2½" wide.

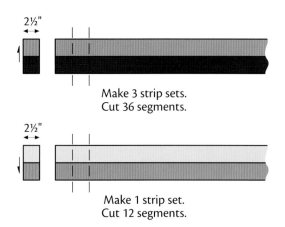

Make 3 strip sets.
Cut 36 segments.

Make 1 strip set.
Cut 12 segments.

❸ Stitch two tan/green segments from step 2 together to make a border four-patch square. Make 6.

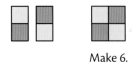

Make 6.

❹ Using four pieced squares from step 1, four green/red segments from step 2, and a light gold 2½" square, sew three rows as shown. Sews the rows together to make a Propeller Block. Make 9.

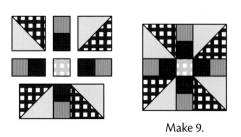

Make 9.

Quilt-Top Assembly and Appliqué

Refer to the assembly diagram for the following steps.

❶ Sew three block rows of three blocks and two light gold 10½"-long sashing strips each. Sew two sashing rows of three sashing strips and two red print 2½" squares each. Sew the rows together.

❷ Stitch red print 1½" x 42" strips to the sides of the quilt top; trim even with the top and bottom. Stitch the remaining red strips to the top and bottom; trim even with the sides.

❸ To make a side pieced border, sew a four-patch square and a red plaid 4½" square to the end of a red plaid 28½" strip. Make two. Sew to the quilt-top sides. Use a red plaid 32½" strip, two four-patch squares, and a red plaid 4½" square to make a top or bottom pieced border. Make two. Sew to the top and bottom.

❹ Referring to the photos and using your favorite technique, position the appliqué shapes in alphabetical order. Appliqué in place.

Quilting and Finishing

Layer, baste, and quilt. Debbie machine echo quilted the appliqué, adding detail lines to the leaves. Block patches are filled with curved-line motifs and the sashing strips filled with continuous curved lines. The inner border is quilted with adjoining circles and the outer border is filled with double rows of scallops. Bind with the bias-cut red plaid strip.

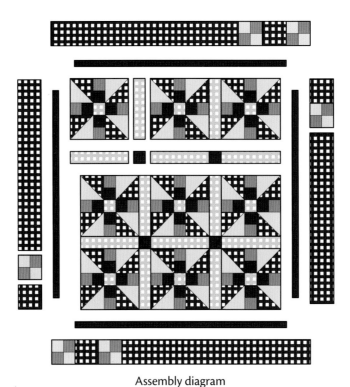

Assembly diagram

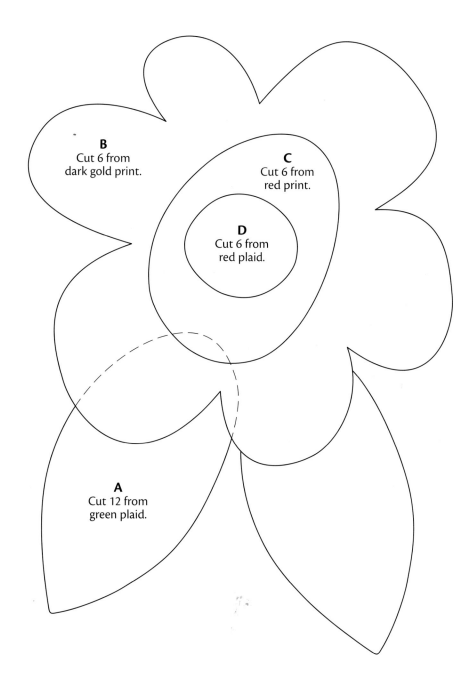

B
Cut 6 from
dark gold print.

C
Cut 6 from
red print.

D
Cut 6 from
red plaid.

A
Cut 12 from
green plaid.

Hot for Dots

JOYCE'S WILD, HAPPY QUILT JUST BURSTS WITH COLOR AND ENERGY! Dots of every color, size, and type dominate the quilt with just a couple of other prints added for variety. This quilt features a pieced binding that continues the confetti feel of the quilt to the very edge. Joyce chose to embellish her pieced binding with a decorative machine stitch using variegated thread.

Finished quilt size: 61" x 90¼"
Number of blocks and finished size:
40 Framed Four Patch blocks, 8" x 8"

Fabric Requirements

- White multicolored polka-dot fabric (blocks, sashing posts, outer border), 2½ yards
- Assorted bright polka-dot fabrics and prints (blocks, binding) , 4¼ to 5¼ yards total
- Black multicolored polka-dot fabric (sashing, inner border), 2⅜ yards
- Backing (piece lengthwise), 5⅝ yards
- Batting, Full size

Cutting Instructions

White multicolored polka-dot fabric:
*2 strips, 5½" x 84", cut on the lengthwise grain
*2 strips, 5½" x 64", cut on the lengthwise grain
80 squares, 2½" x 2½"
28 squares, 2¼" x 2¼"

Assorted bright polka-dot fabrics and prints:
40 matching sets of 8 squares, 2½" x 2½"
40 matching sets of 2 rectangles, 2½" x 4½", and
    2 strips, 2½" x 6½"
10 total strips, 2½" x 42"

Black multicolored polka-dot fabric:
*2 strips, 2¼" x 80", cut on the lengthwise grain
*2 strips, 2¼" x 55", cut on the lengthwise grain
67 strips, 2¼" x 8½"

*Cut first.

Piecing the Blocks

❶ Each block uses one set of eight matching bright 2½" squares, one contrasting matching set of two bright rectangles and strips, plus two white 2½" squares. Sew two matching bright 2½" squares to two white 2½" squares as shown. Sew the rows together to make a four-patch unit. Make 40 total.

Make 40 total.

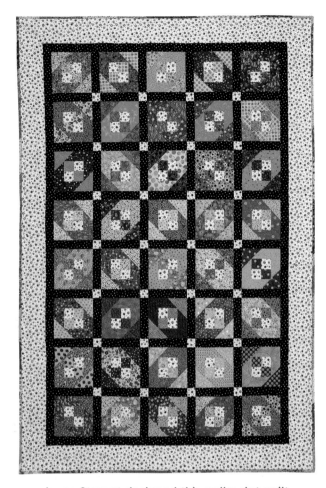

Joyce Stewart designed this polka-dot quilt
that promises start-to-finish fun!

❷ Draw a diagonal line on the wrong side of a matching
bright 2½" square. Place the square on a contrasting
bright 2½" x 4½" rectangle, right sides together and raw
edges aligned. Stitch on the drawn line. Trim away and
discard the excess fabric; press open to make a pieced
rectangle. Make 40 sets of two matching units.

Make 40 sets
of 2 matching units.

❸ Draw a diagonal line on the wrong side of a matching
bright 2½" square. Place the square on a contrasting
bright 2½" x 6½" strip, right sides together and raw edges
aligned. Stitch on the drawn line. Trim away and discard
the excess fabric; press open. Sew a matching 2½" square
to the end to make a pieced strip. Make 40 sets of two
matching units.

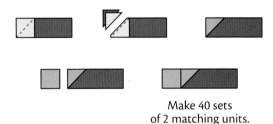

Make 40 sets
of 2 matching units.

❹ Sew matching pieced rectangles from step 2 to the
sides of the four-patch units.

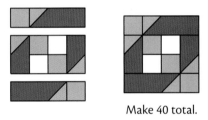

❺ Stitch matching pieced strips from step 3 to the top
and bottom of the units to make Framed Four Patch
blocks. Make 40 total.

Make 40 total.

Quilt-Top Assembly

❶ Referring to the assembly diagram, stitch eight block
rows using five blocks and four black 2¼" x 8½" strips
each, rotating the blocks as shown. Stitch seven sashing
rows using five black 8½"-long strips and four white 2¼"
squares each. Sew the rows together as shown.

❷ Sew the black inner and white outer borders to the quilt top, adding the side strips first for each border, and then the top and bottom strips. Trim after each addition.

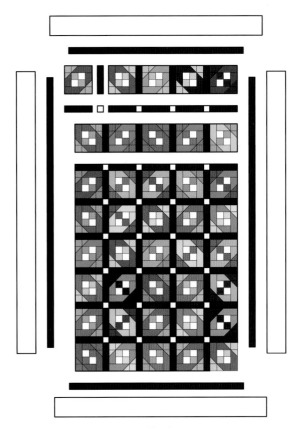

Assembly diagram

Quilting and Finishing

❶ Layer, baste, and quilt. Joyce machine quilted a circle-and-loop motif in each block and meandering loops in the sashing. Crescent moons and stars are quilted in the border.

❷ To make the pieced binding, cut the assorted bright 2½" x 42" strips into random lengths from 4" to 12" as desired. Sew the strips together as shown. Bind the quilt with the pieced strip. If desired, sew along the binding seam with a decorative stitch using variegated thread.

Trim and
press open.

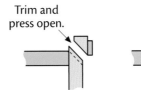

QUEEN-SIZE OPTION

Finished quilt size: 80½" x 100"
Number of blocks and finished size: 63 Framed Four Patch blocks, 8" x 8"

Fabric Requirements

- White multicolored polka-dot fabric, 2¾ yards

- Assorted bright polka-dot fabrics and prints, 6 to 7 yards *total*

- Black multicolored polka-dot fabric, 2⅝ yards

- Backing (piece widthwise), 7½ yards

- Batting, Queen size

Construction

Following the instructions for the featured quilt on page 18, make 63 blocks. Refer to the assembly diagram for steps 1 and 2.

❶ Sew nine block rows of seven blocks and six black 8½" strips each. Sew eight sashing rows of seven black 8½" strips and six white 2¼" squares each. Sew the rows together as shown.

❷ Stitch the borders to the quilt top, adding the side strips first for each border, and then the top and bottom strips. Trim after each addition.

❸ Layer, baste, and quilt. Make the pieced binding using 12 assorted bright 2½" x 42" strips and following the instructions on page 95. Bind with the pieced strip.

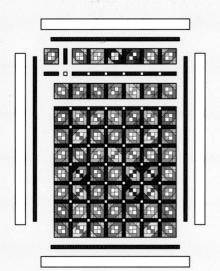

Queen-size assembly diagram

Simply Fabulous

THE ASSORTED FLORALS AND PRINTS IN NANCY'S BLOCKS include a variety of colors—greens, browns, golds, and beiges—and range in value from light to dark. An easy method for choosing a palette for your block fabrics is to first choose the border fabric and use it as guide when selecting block fabrics. Be sure to select a variety of values, and include fabrics that aren't a perfect match—they add interest to the quilt!

Finished quilt size: 60" x 60"
Number of blocks and finished size:
36 Simply Fabulous blocks, 7¼" x 7¼"

Fabric Requirements

- Assorted florals and prints (blocks), 2 to 2½ yards *total*

- Cream print (blocks), ¾ yard

- Red print (blocks), 10" x 10" piece

- Dark green print (sashing, inner border, binding), 1½ yards

- Light green print (sashing posts), 10" x 10" piece

- Cream large-scale floral (outer border), 2 yards

- Backing, 4 yards

- Batting, Twin size

Cutting Instructions

Assorted florals and prints:
36 sets of 4 matching squares, 3¾" x 3¾" (144 total)

Cream print:
144 strips, 1¼" x 3¾"

Red print:
36 squares, 1¼" x 1¼"

Dark green print:
7 strips, 2½" x 42"
*4 strips, 1½" x 54", pieced from 6 strips, 42" long
60 strips, 1½" x 7¾"

Light green print:
25 squares, 1½" x 1½"

Cream large-scale floral:
4 strips, 5" x 64", cut on the lengthwise grain

Cut first.

Quilt-Top Assembly

❶ Make 36 Simply Fabulous blocks as shown.

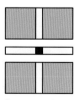

Make 36 total.

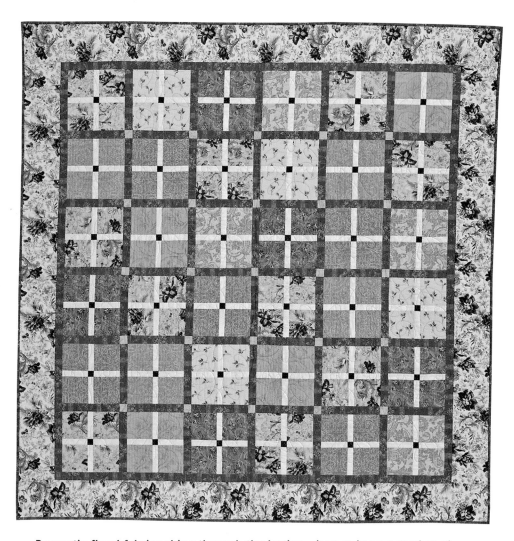

Romantic floral fabrics shine through the lattice—just as in an actual garden—
in this beauty designed by Nancy Mahoney.

❷ Refer to the assembly diagram for the following steps.
Sew six block rows using six blocks and five dark green
strips each. Stitch five sashing rows using six dark green
strips and five light green squares each. Sew the rows
together.

❸ Stitch dark green 1½" x 54" strips to the sides of the
quilt top; trim even with the top and bottom. Stitch the
remaining dark green strips to the top and bottom; trim
even with the sides. Sew cream floral strips to the sides;
trim. Stitch the remaining cream floral strips to the top and
bottom; trim.

Quilting and Finishing

Layer, baste, and quilt. Nancy machine quilted an overall
looping pattern. Bind with dark green print.

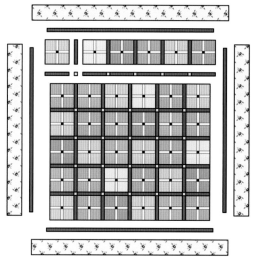

Lap-sized assembly diagram

QUEEN-SIZE OPTION

Finished quilt size: 86¾" x 95"
Number of blocks and finished size: 90 Simply
Fabulous blocks, 7¼" x 7¼"

Fabric Requirements

- Assorted florals and prints, 4 to 4¼ yards *total*

- Cream print, 1⅜ yards

- Red print, ¼ yard

- Dark green print, 2¾ yards

- Light green print, ¼ yard

- Cream large-scale floral, 2¾ yards

- Backing (piece widthwise), 8⅛ yards

- Batting size, King

Construction

Following the instructions for the featured quilt on page
22, make 90 total blocks. Refer to the assembly diagram
for steps 1 and 2.

❶ Sew 10 block rows using nine blocks and eight dark
green strips each. Stitch nine sashing rows using nine
green strips and eight light green squares each. Sew the
rows together.

❷ Stitch dark green 86"-long strips to the sides; trim
even with the top and bottom. Stitch the remaining green
strips to the top and bottom; trim even with the sides.
Sew cream floral strips to the sides; trim. Stitch the
remaining cream floral strips to the top and bottom; trim.

❸ Layer, baste, and quilt. Bind with the dark green
print.

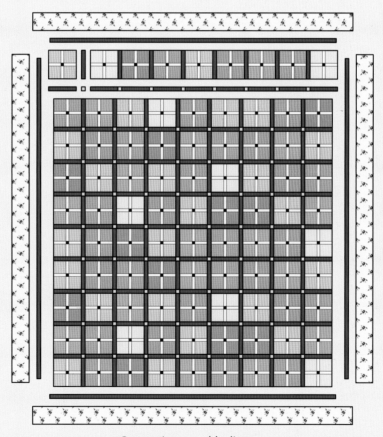

Queen-size assembly diagram

Cherry Lime Phosphate

Fabric fat quarters are so much fun to collect, display, and use in quilting. This bright, cheerful design makes the most of "fats" with creative cutting and easy piecing. Like a cold fountain drink on a warm day, it's a pure, refreshing treat

Finished quilt size: 59½" x 76⅜"
Number of blocks and finished size: 17 Nine Patch Variation blocks, 8" x 8"

Fabric Requirements

- Assorted pink and green prints, 18 fat quarters *total**
- Assorted white prints, 3 fat quarters *total**
- Dark pink polka-dot fabric (inner border), ½ yard
- Lime polka-dot fabric (outer border), 1 yard
- Pink-and-white polka-dot fabric (binding), ¾ yard
- Backing (piece lengthwise), 4¾ yards
- Batting, Twin size

*A fat quarter is an 18" x 20" to 22" cut of fabric. We recommend you not prewash the fabrics for this quilt, because the fat-quarter cutting plans require a minimum size of 18" x 20" each.

Fat-Quarter Cutting

Susan and Mary Jane made cutting the fat-quarter fabrics almost as much fun as sewing them! Follow these easy steps to cut all your fat quarters:

❶ Measure and mark each of the 18 assorted pink and green and three of the white fat quarters as shown.

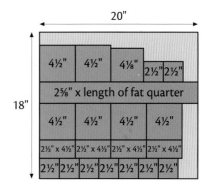

Assorted pink and green prints

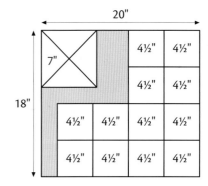

Assorted white prints

**Setting the blocks on point adds an air of jauntiness to this design by
Mary Jane Mattingly and Susan Knapp of The Quilt Branch.**

❷ Cut the pink and green fat quarters in strips.

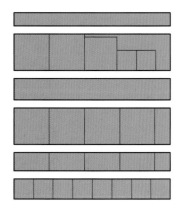

❸ Cut apart the pink and green squares and rectangles. Discard the fabric from the areas shaded gray in the cutting diagram (step 1).

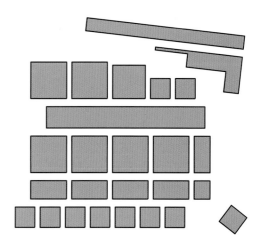

❹ In a similar manner, cut the marked white fat quarters into strips, and then into squares. Cut the 7" square into quarters diagonally as shown in the cutting diagram (step 1). Discard the excess fabric.

❺ Mark and trim the pink and green $4\frac{1}{2}$" squares to create sashing units as shown.

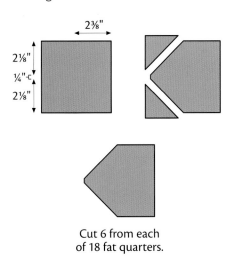

Cut 6 from each
of 18 fat quarters.

❻ Mark and cut each $2\frac{5}{8}$" strip into six $5\frac{1}{4}$" triangles as shown.

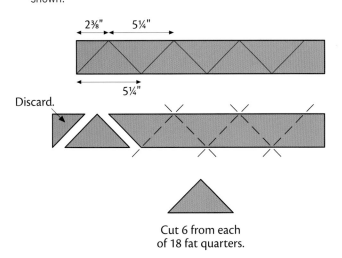

Cut 6 from each
of 18 fat quarters.

❼ For 16 of the pink and green fabrics, mark and cut the $4\frac{1}{8}$" squares into quarters diagonally to make four quarter-square triangles each as shown.

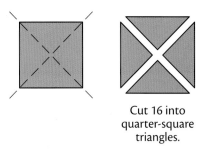

Cut 16 into
quarter-square
triangles.

❽ For the remaining two pink and green fabrics, mark and cut the $4\frac{1}{8}$" squares in half diagonally to make two half-square triangles each as shown.

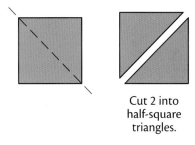

Cut 2 into
half-square
triangles.

Border and Binding Cutting

See "Fat-Quarter Cutting" on page 26 for the cutting instructions for the fat quarters.

Dark pink polka-dot fabric:
2 strips, $1\frac{1}{2}$" x 72", pieced from 4 strips, 42" long
2 strips, $1\frac{1}{2}$" x 58", pieced from 3 strips, 42" long

Lime polka-dot fabric:
4 strips, $3\frac{1}{2}$" x 74", pieced from 8 strips, 42" long

Pink-and-white polka-dot fabric:
7 strips, $2\frac{1}{2}$" x 42"

Piecing the Blocks and Units

❶ Sew assorted $2\frac{1}{2}$" squares to both ends of assorted $2\frac{1}{2}$" x $4\frac{1}{2}$" rectangles as shown. Make 34 total.

Make 34 total.

❷ Sew assorted 2½" x 4½" rectangles to both sides of white print 4½" squares as shown. Make 17 total.

Make 17 total.

❸ Sew the units from steps 1 and 2 together to make Nine Patch Variation blocks as shown. Make 17 total.

Make 17 total.

❹ Sew trimmed assorted 4½" squares (previously cut in "Fat-Quarter Cutting," step 4) to assorted 5¼" triangles (previously cut in "Fat-Quarter Cutting," step 5) as shown. Make 96 total.

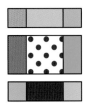

Make 96 total.

❺ Sew two units from step 4 together to make a sashing unit as shown. Make 48 total.

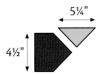

Make 48 total.

❻ Sew assorted 2½" squares and assorted 4⅛" quarter-square triangles together into rows as shown. Sew the rows together to make a pieced setting triangle. Make 14 total.

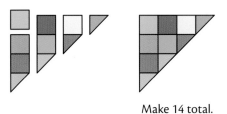

Make 14 total.

Quilt-Top Assembly, Quilting, and Finishing

❶ Referring to the assembly diagram, stitch 13 diagonal rows using the pieced setting triangles, sashing units, white 7" quarter-square triangles, white 4½" squares, and blocks. Sew the rows together. Sew the assorted 4⅛" half-square triangles to the corners. Trim all edges even.

❷ Stitch the dark pink polka-dot 72"-long strips to the quilt-top sides; trim even with the top and bottom. Stitch the remaining dark pink strips to the top and bottom; trim even with the sides. Sew lime strips to the sides; trim. Sew the remaining lime strips to the top and bottom; trim.

❸ Layer, baste, and quilt. Mary machine quilted a continuous swirl pattern across the quilt. Bind with the pink-and-white polka-dot fabric.

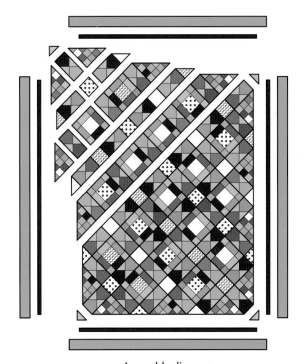

Assembly diagram

Get Creative and Try a New Colorway!

This pattern looks great in lots of fabric themes. Here are three in different fabric colorways to give your creativity a jump start.

Basically Batik

THIS BEAUTIFUL QUILT LOOKS VERY INTRICATE AND COMPLEX, but the cutting and sewing is really quite simple. Essentially, this quilt uses just one block stitched in three different sizes. Notice that the light batiks are always on the sides of the blocks, while the dark batiks are on the top and bottom. Follow the illustrations carefully to ensure that your light and dark batik pieces are positioned properly.

Finished quilt size: $36\frac{1}{2}$" x $48\frac{1}{2}$"

Number of blocks and finished sizes: 68 Hourglass blocks, 3" x 3"; 16 Hourglass blocks, $4\frac{1}{2}$" x $4\frac{1}{2}$"; and 22 Hourglass blocks, 6" x 6"

Fabric Requirements

- Assorted light batiks (blocks), $1\frac{5}{8}$ to $2\frac{1}{4}$ yards *total*

- Assorted dark batiks (blocks), $1\frac{5}{8}$ to $2\frac{1}{4}$ yards *total*

- Dark blue batik (binding), $\frac{5}{8}$ yard

- Backing (piece widthwise), $2\frac{5}{8}$ yards

- Batting, Crib size

Cutting Instructions

Assorted light batiks—cut a *total* of:

*11 squares, $7\frac{1}{4}$" x $7\frac{1}{4}$"

*8 squares, $5\frac{3}{4}$" x $5\frac{3}{4}$"

34 squares, $4\frac{1}{4}$" x $4\frac{1}{4}$"

Assorted dark batiks—cut a *total* of:

*11 squares, $7\frac{1}{4}$" x $7\frac{1}{4}$"

*8 squares, $5\frac{3}{4}$" x $5\frac{3}{4}$"

34 squares, $4\frac{1}{4}$" x $4\frac{1}{4}$"

Dark blue batik:

5 strips, $2\frac{1}{2}$" x 42"

Cut first.

Piecing the Blocks

❶ On wrong side of one light batik $4\frac{1}{4}$" square, draw two diagonal lines. Place the marked square on dark batik $4\frac{1}{4}$" square, right sides together. Sew $\frac{1}{4}$" seam on each side of one line. Cut on the drawn lines as shown, cutting the sewn square into quarters. Press open to make small pieced triangles. Repeat with all 34 squares to make 136 total.

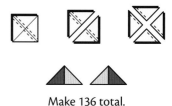

Make 136 total.

❷ In same manner, use light and dark batik $5\frac{3}{4}$" squares to make 32 total medium pieced triangles.

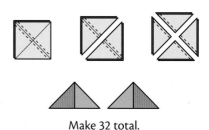

Make 32 total.

Simple blocks and beautiful batiks combine to make Hourglass art! Designed by Kay M. Capps Cross.

❸ Repeat with light and dark batik 7¼" squares to make 44 total large pieced triangles.

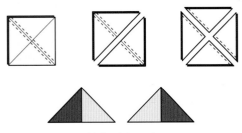

Make 44 total.

❹ Stitch two pieced triangles of the same size together as shown. Make 68 small, 16 medium, and 22 large Hourglass Blocks total.

Make 68 total.

Make 16 total.

Make 22 total.

❺ Sew four medium and seven small Hourglass Blocks together to make unit A as shown. Make four total.

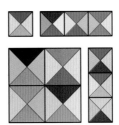
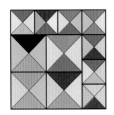

Unit A.
Make 4 total.

❻ Sew four large Hourglass blocks together to make unit B as shown. Make three total.

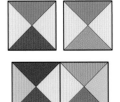
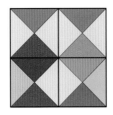

Unit B.
Make 3 total.

❼ Sew eight small and two large Hourglass blocks together to make unit C as shown. Make five total.

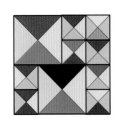
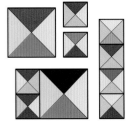

Unit C.
Make 5 total.

Quilt-Top Assembly, Quilting, and Finishing

❶ Referring to the assembly diagram, stitch units A, B, and C together to make three sections. Stitch the sections together.

❷ Layer, baste, and quilt. Kay machine quilted zigzags and concentric diamonds in the light patches and spirals and leaf sprays in the dark patches. Bind with the dark blue batik.

Section 1   Section 2   Section 3

Assembly diagram

Domino

CORI AND MYRA'S CUTE DESIGN is a great way to show off bright, large-scale cotton prints. These domino blocks let you stack up a cool contemporary look in no time at all. You'll have a fast, fun way to incorporate lots of color and pattern into any room's decor!

Finished quilt size: 56½" x 68½"
Number of blocks and finished size:
16 Domino blocks, 9" x 12"

Fabric Requirements

- Black solid fabric (blocks, border, binding) 2⅞ yards

- 8 assorted bright prints (blocks), 1 fat quarter* *each*

- White solid fabric (sashing), 1⅛ yards

- Backing (piece widthwise), 3¾ yards

- Batting, Twin size

- Paper-backed fusible web, 1 yard

A fat quarter is an 18" x 20" to 22" cut of fabric.

Cutting Instructions

The circle pattern, printed without a seam allowance for paper-backed fusible web, is on page 38.

Black solid fabric:
*4 strips, 5½" x 62", cut on the lengthwise grain
*5 strips, 2½" x 60", cut on the lengthwise grain (binding)
32 strips, 1½" x 10½"
32 strips, 1½" x 9½"

8 assorted bright prints—cut from *each* fat quarter:
2 rectangles, 7½" x 10½" (16 total)

White solid fabric:
*5 strips, 2½" x 50", pieced from 7 strips, 42"
20 strips, 2½" x 12½"

Cut first.

Making the Blocks

❶ Sew black 10½"-long strips to the sides of an assorted bright rectangle. Sew black 9½"-long strips to top and bottom. Make 16 total pieced rectangles.

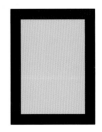

Make 16 total.

❷ Trace the pattern circles on the paper side of paper-backed fusible web. Cut apart, leaving a small margin beyond the drawn lines. Following the manufacturer's instructions, fuse to the wrong side of the black solid; cut out on the drawn lines.

❸ Finger-press a pieced rectangle in half lengthwise and widthwise; use the folds as a placement guide. Position two black circles on the pieced rectangle. Following the manufacturer's instructions, fuse in place.

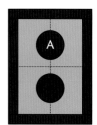

Make 16 total.

❹ Machine or hand blanket stitch the circle edges. Repeat to make 16 Domino blocks.

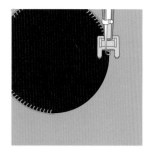

Quilt-Top Assembly

Refer to the assembly diagram for the following steps.

❶ To make a block row, sew five white 12½"-long strips and four blocks together as shown. Make four rows total. Sew the white 50"-long strips and the block rows together, alternating and trimming the white strips after each addition.

❷ Sew black 62"-long strips to the sides; trim even with the top and bottom. Sew the remaining black 62"-long strips to the top and bottom; trim even with the sides.

❸ Layer, baste, and quilt. Karen machine quilted the print rectangles and black circles in the ditch. The rectangles are filled with assorted motifs. The blocks are outline stitched in white, and a straight line is quilted ¼" from the outer edge of the white sashing. The black border strips feature a centered line of continuous assorted circles. Bind with the black solid strips.

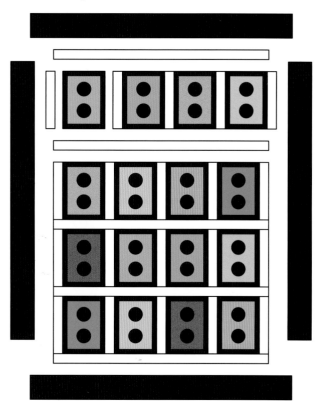

Assembly diagram

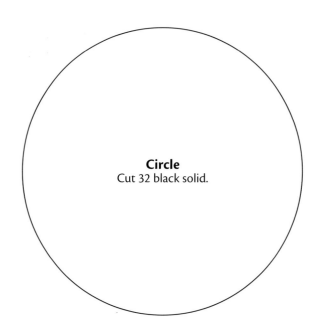

Circle
Cut 32 black solid.

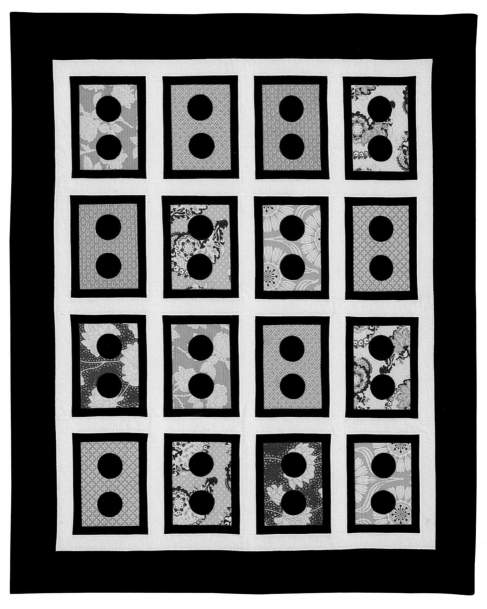

This quick and modern quilt designed by Cori Derksen and Myra Harder
is sure to please. Machine quilted by Karen Greaves.

Pathway to Nowhere

ELAINE McGARRY PROFESSES, "I AM A REPRODUCTION QUILTER. Since quilters in the 1800s had to use whatever fabrics were available to them, there were a lot of scrap quilts made from old dresses and clothing. I think scrap quilts are so much more interesting, and when replicating the look of an antique quilt, I get to use so many more fabrics!"

Finished quilt size: 91" x 107"
Number of blocks and finished size:
120 Single Chain blocks, 8" x 8"

Fabric Requirements

- Cream print (blocks, inner border), 2 yards

- Black print (blocks, outer border, binding), 4⅜ yards

- *Assorted medium and dark prints (blocks), 6 to 6½ yards *total*

- Backing (piece widthwise), 8⅜ yards

- Batting, King size

The featured quilt was made with 120 different medium and dark prints to enhance the scrappy appearance. If you prefer, you can use 30 fat quarters of medium and dark prints (a fat quarter is an 18" x 20" to 22" cut of fabric) or a true quarter of a yard. Each fat quarter will make 4 matching blocks.

Cutting Instructions

Cream print:
37 strips, 1½" x 42"
2 strips, 1" x 100", pieced from 5 strips, 42" long
2 strips, 1" x 86", pieced from 5 strips, 42" long

Black print:
37 strips, 1½" x 42"
2 strips, 5½" x 102", pieced from 5 strips, 42" long
2 strips, 5½" x 96", pieced from 5 strips, 42" long
10 strips, 2½" x 42"

Assorted medium and dark prints—cut 120 *matching sets* of:
4 squares, 2½" x 2½" (480 total)
2 squares, 4½" x 4½" (240 total)

Piecing the Blocks

❶ Sew cream and black 1½" x 42" strips together as shown; press toward the black strips. Make 37. From the pieced strips, cut 960 segments, 1½" wide.

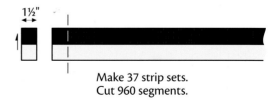

Make 37 strip sets.
Cut 960 segments.

Whether stitched in reproduction or modern fabrics, Elaine McGarry's
design will be a scrappy delight.

❷ Sew two segments together to make a four-patch unit as shown. Make 480.

Make 480.

❸ Sew two rows using two four-patch units and two matching assorted print 2½" squares, watching placement and orientation. Sew the rows together to make double four-patch units. Make 120 sets of two matching units (240 total).

Make 120 sets
of 2 matching units.

❹ Sew two matching units and two matching 4½" squares together to make a Single Chain Block. Repeat to make 120 total.

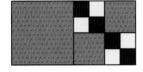

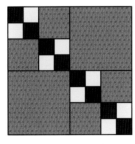

Make 120 total.

Quilt-Top Assembly

Refer to the assembly diagram for the following steps.

❶ Sew 12 rows of 10 blocks each, rotating the blocks as shown. Stitch the rows together.

❷ Sew the cream 100"-long strips to the sides; trim even with the top and bottom. Sew the cream 86"-long strips to the top and bottom; trim even with the sides. Sew the black 102"-long strips to the sides; trim even. Sew the black 96"-long strips to the top and bottom; trim even.

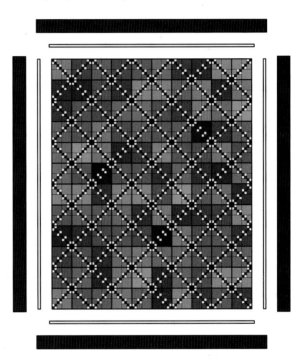

Quilting and Finishing

Layer, baste, and quilt. Elaine quilted feathered wreaths in the medium and dark print areas between the chains and small feathered circles where the black and white four-patch units meet. The borders are quilted with a feathered vine pattern. Bind with the black print strips.

Searching

"I LOVE SEARCHING THROUGH MY STASH AND SCRAP FABRICS and finding the perfect pieces for a scrap quilt," Joanne says. "It is like a walk down memory lane . . . remembering the shopping trip when the fabric was purchased, who gave me the fabric, or another quilt the fabric was used in. Scrap quilts . . . these are the best quilts."

Finished quilt size: 45½" x 63½"
Number of blocks and finished size: 24 blocks, 9" x 9"

Fabric Requirements

- *Assorted tan and cream prints (blocks), 1⅝ to 2 yards *total*

- Assorted red prints (blocks), 1 to 1¼ yards *total*

- Assorted blue prints (blocks, pieced binding), 1½ to 1¾ yards *total*

- Blue striped fabric (inner border), ⅜ yard

- Red-and-tan print (outer border), ⅞ yard

- Backing (piece widthwise), 3⅛ yards

- Batting, Twin size

Make sure your tan and cream fabric selections have small red or blue motifs printed on them to pull the color palette of this quilt together.

Cutting Instructions

Assorted tan and cream prints—cut a *total* of:
72 squares, 3⅞" x 3⅞"; cut each square in half diagonally to make 144 half-square triangles
144 squares, 2⅜" x 2⅜"; cut each square in half diagonally to make 288 half-square triangles

Assorted red prints—cut a *total* of:
12 squares, 7¼" x 7¼"; cut each square into quarters diagonally to make 48 quarter-square triangles
18 squares, 4¼" x 4¼"; cut each square into quarters diagonally to make 72 quarter-square triangles

Assorted blue prints—cut a *total* of:
*7 strips, 2½" x 42"
6 squares, 7¼" x 7¼"; cut each square into quarters diagonally to make 24 quarter-square triangles
18 squares, 4¼" x 4¼"; cut each square into quarters diagonally to make 72 quarter-square triangles

Blue striped fabric:
2 strips, 1½" x 58", pieced from 3 strips, 42" long
2 strips, 1½" x 42", pieced from 3 strips, 42" long

Red-and-tan print:
4 strips, 4" x 60", pieced from 6 strips, 42" long

Cut first.

Search your stash for as many reds, blues, and creams as you can find. Or visit your
local quilt shop for an array of fat quarters to make this fun Flying Geese quilt.
Designed by Joanne Rowicki. Machine quilted by Jeanine Drzewiecki.

Piecing the Blocks

1 Sew half-square triangles to the sides of quarter-square triangles to make flying-geese units in the sizes, color combinations, and quantities shown.

   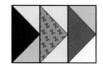

Make 48 total. Make 24 total.

Make 72 total. Make 72 total.

2 Sew two red and one blue large flying-geese unit together to make a pieced rectangle. Make 24 total.

Make 24 total.

3 Stitch three red and three blue small flying-geese units together to make a pieced strip. Make 24 total.

Make 24 total.

4 Stitch a pieced rectangle and a pieced strip together to make a block. Make 24 total.

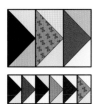 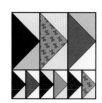

Make 24 total.

Quilt-Top Assembly

Refer to the assembly diagram for the following steps.

1 Sew six rows of four blocks each, rotating the blocks as shown. Sew the rows together.

2 Stitch the blue striped 58"-long strips to the sides; trim even with the top and bottom. Stitch the blue striped 42"-long strips to the top and bottom; trim even with the sides. Sew red-and-tan strips to the sides; trim even. Sew the remaining red-and-tan strips to the top and bottom; trim even.

Assembly diagram

Quilting and Finishing

1 Layer, baste, and quilt. Jeanine machine quilted with tan thread in an overall swirling pattern.

2 Cut assorted blue 42"-long strips into 18" to 22" segments. Sew the segments together end to end using diagonal seams as shown. Trim the corners and discard the excess fabric. Press the seam allowances open. Press the pieced strip in half lengthwise, wrong sides together. Bind the quilt with the pieced strip.

Trim and press open.

Americana Home

BY USING FOUR MATCHING JELLY ROLLS (each with 40 precut 2½"-wide fabric strips), you can reduce your fabric-cutting time considerably. However, if you prefer to work from your stash, you can substitute leftover strips or use ⅓ yard each of 16 light prints and 16 dark prints and cut four 2½"-wide strips from each.

Finished quilt size: 72½" x 88½"
Number of blocks and finished size: 99 blocks, 8" x 8"

Fabric Requirements

- *Jelly Rolls (blocks, binding), 4 matching

- Backing (piece lengthwise), 5½ yards

- Batting, Full size

*Jelly Rolls are bundles of precut 2½"-wide fabric strips, generally containing about 40 strips each. Divide the fabric strips from each Jelly Roll into 3 groups: 16 light strips, 16 dark strips, and 8 strips left over. Combine all the light groups for 64 assorted light strips and all dark groups for 64 assorted dark strips. Of the leftover strips, 9 will be used for binding the quilt and 23 can be used for other projects.

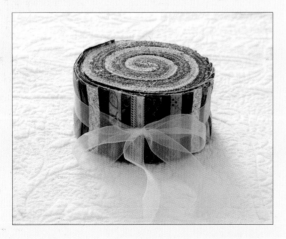

Cutting Instructions

*Assorted light strips—cut a *total* of:
196 squares, 2½" x 2½"
98 strips, 2½" x 8½"

*Assorted dark strips—cut a *total* of:
200 squares, 2½" x 2½"
100 strips, 2½" x 8½"

Set aside 26 total 2½" x 42" strips from this group for step 1 before cutting other pieces.

Piecing the Blocks

❶ Sew two assorted light 42"-long strips together as shown. Make 13 total. Press the seam allowances toward the darker fabrics. From the strips, cut 50 segments, 8½" each. In same manner, make 13 total assorted dark strip sets and cut 49 total segments.

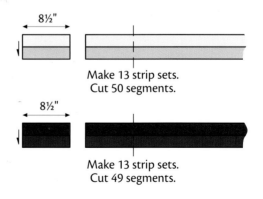

Make 13 strip sets.
Cut 50 segments.

Make 13 strip sets.
Cut 49 segments.

❷ Draw a diagonal line on the wrong side of an assorted dark 2½" square. Place the marked square on an assorted light segment, right sides together, aligning the raw edges. Sew on the marked line; trim away and discard the excess fabric. Press open. Repeat on the remaining corners to make a pieced rectangle. Make 50 total. In the same manner, make 49 total pieced rectangles using assorted light squares and assorted dark segments.

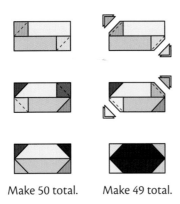

Make 50 total.   Make 49 total.

❸ Complete 99 total blocks in the fabric arrangements and quantities shown.

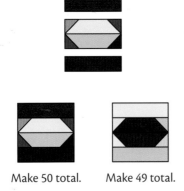

Make 50 total.   Make 49 total.

Quilt-Top Assembly and Finishing

❶ Sew 11 rows of nine blocks each, alternating and watching the orientation of the blocks. Sew the rows together.

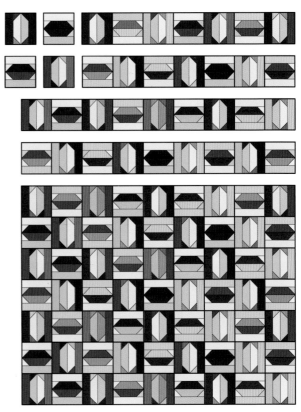

Assembly diagram

❷ Layer, baste, and quilt. Nancy machine quilted a continuous flower and leaf design in variegated blue thread.

❸ Sew nine leftover assorted 42"-long strips together end to end using diagonal seams as shown. Bind the quilt with the pieced strip.

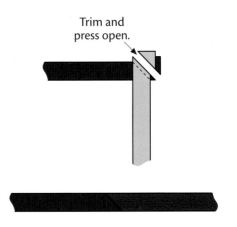

Trim and
press open.

Using a Jelly Roll to make a scrappy quilt is so easy and fun!
Designed by Lisa Christensen. Machine quilted by Nancy Wines of Calico Station.

Lunar Eclipse

USING SMALL FABRIC CUTS LIKE FAT EIGHTHS assures a scrappy mix of colors and textures in this engaging quilt. *McCall's Quilting* art director Ellie Brown chose batiks for her block fabrics. Our how-to illustrations take the mystery out of circular piecing.

Finished quilt size: 48½" x 64½"
Number of blocks and finished size:
48 Circle blocks, 8" x 8"

Fabric Requirements

- Assorted batiks (blocks), 40 to 44 fat eighths* *total*

- Brown-and-green mottled print (binding), ⅝ yard

- Backing (piece widthwise), 3¼ yards

- Batting, Twin size

- Freezer paper

- Removable fabric pencil

A fat eighth is a 9" x 20" to 22" cut of fabric.

Cutting Instructions

The circle pattern, printed without a seam allowance for paper-backed fusible web, is on page 56.

Assorted batiks—cut a *total* of:
48 squares, 6" x 6"
48 squares, 9" x 9"

Brown-and-green mottled print:
6 strips, 2½" x 42"

Freezer paper:
*9" x 9" squares

Freezer paper patterns are reusable several times. Cut squares as needed.

Piecing the Blocks

❶ Finger-press a 9" square of freezer paper in half on both length and width. Make a template from the pattern on page 56. Trace the circle template on the dull side of the freezer-paper square, centering the circle.

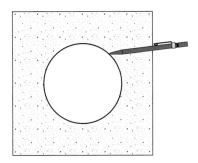

❷ Mark hatch marks at approximately 1" intervals around the circle, making sure each mark crosses the traced line from the inside to the outside of the circle. At one hatch mark, make two additional lines. Carefully cut out the circle on the traced line.

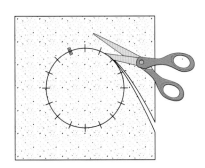

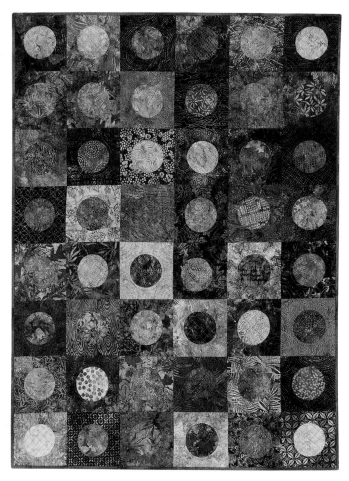

Scrappy circles in both warm and cool colors make this batik quilt shine. Designed by Ellie Brown. Machine quilted by Laura Gerse, Custom Stitches Longarm Machine Quilting.

❸ Finger-press an assorted 6" square in half on both length and width. Press the shiny side of the freezer-paper circle to the wrong side of the fabric using the fold lines to center. Press the shiny side of the freezer-paper square (with the center circle cut out) to the wrong side of an assorted 9" square.

❹ To prepare a fabric circle for piecing, use a removable fabric pencil to trace around the freezer-paper circle. Transfer the hatch marks to the fabric.

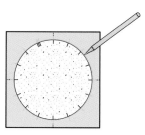

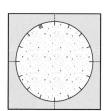 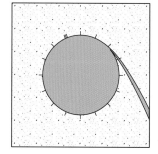

❺ Cut out, adding approximately ¼" for seam allowance. Remove freezer paper.

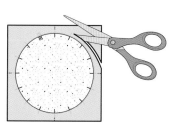

6 To prepare the fabric square for piecing, trace around the cut-out circle, transfer the hatch marks to the fabric, and then cut out the fabric center circle, adding approximately ¼" seam allowance inside the marked line. Remove the freezer paper. Make a ⅛" clip in the seam allowance between each pair of hatch marks.

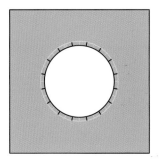

7 Pin the prepared square to the circle, right sides together, matching hatch marks starting at the triple line marking and aligning the drawn circle lines.

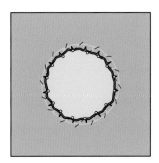

8 Sew together on the line, keeping the circle on the bottom.

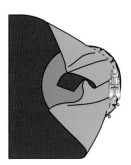

9 Press the seam allowances toward the center. Trim the Circle block to 8½" square, centering the circle. Repeat steps 3 through 6 to make 48 total Circle blocks.

Quilt-Top Assembly, Quilting, and Finishing

1 Sew eight rows of six blocks each. Sew the rows together.

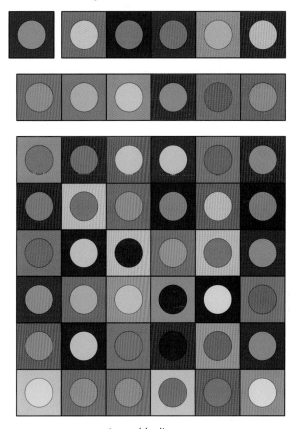

Assembly diagram

2 Layer, baste, and quilt. Laura machine outline quilted the circles and filled them with diagonal grids (stitching lines approximately ⅞" apart). Six concentric circles are stitched in each space where four blocks join (with stitching lines ½" apart). Partial concentric circles are stitched along the outside edge of the quilt. Bind the quilt with the brown-and-green mottled print.

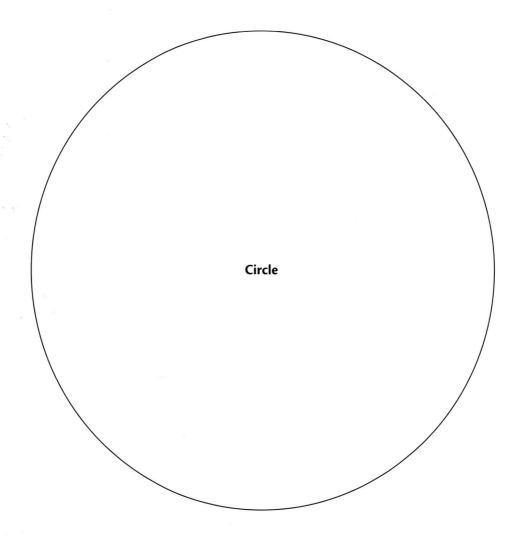

Circle

Lattice Garden

YOU CAN ACHIEVE A SWEET, SCRAPPY LOOK by using a bundle of smaller cuts of fabric. Glenna designed this cheerful quilt using a "Sweet Sixteen swirl" of her Bee's Knees fabric collection by Maywood Studios. Rickrack vines add a touch of whimsy and 1940's style.

On a wall or as a table topper, this cheerful design by Glenna Hailey
is sure to make you smile. Machine quilted by Mary M. Covey.

Finished quilt size: $48\frac{1}{2}$" x $48\frac{1}{2}$"

Number of blocks and finished size:
36 Lattice blocks, 6" x 6"

Fabric Requirements

- 36 assorted prints (blocks, leaves), 1 Sweet Sixteen *each**

- White-on-white print (blocks), $1\frac{1}{4}$ yards

- Gold print (inner border), $\frac{3}{8}$ yard

- Blue daisy print (outer border, binding), $1\frac{5}{8}$ yards

- Backing, $3\frac{1}{4}$ yards

- Batting, Twin size

- Gold, blue, red, and green medium ($\frac{1}{2}$") rickrack $1\frac{1}{2}$ yards *each*

*A Sweet Sixteen ($\frac{1}{16}$ yard) is a 9" x 10" to 11" cut of fabric. To substitute, buy $\frac{1}{4}$ yard (which is 9" wide) and cut into 3 or 4 pieces.

Cutting Instructions

The leaf pattern, printed without a seam allowance for paper-backed fusible web, is on page 59.

36 assorted prints:
Cut from each:
  2 squares, 2" x 2" (72 total)
  1 square, $3\frac{7}{8}$" x $3\frac{7}{8}$" (36 total)
Cut a total of:
  76 using leaf template

White-on-white print:
72 squares, 2" x 2"
36 squares, $3\frac{7}{8}$" x $3\frac{7}{8}$"
36 squares, $3\frac{1}{2}$" x $3\frac{1}{2}$"

Gold print:
4 strips, 2" x 42"

Blue daisy print
4 strips, 5" x 52", cut on the lengthwise grain
5 strips, $2\frac{1}{2}$" x 42"

Piecing the Blocks

❶ Use two matching print and two white 2" squares to make a four-patch unit. Make 36 total.

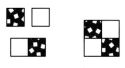

Make 36 total.

❷ Draw a diagonal line on the wrong side of a white 3⅞" square. Place the marked square on a print 3⅞" square, right sides together. Sew ¼" from each side of the marked line; cut apart on the marked line. Press open to make two pieced squares. Make 36 sets of two matching squares.

Make 36 sets
of 2 matching squares.

❸ Use a matching four-patch unit, two pieced squares, and a white 3½" square to make a Lattice Block. Make 36 total.

Make 36 total.

Quilt-Top Assembly and Appliqué

❶ Sew six rows of six blocks each, rotating as shown. Sew the rows together.

❷ Cut rickrack vines as follows: one length of 16" and one of 26" from gold; one length of 35" from blue; one length of 53" from red; and one length of 46" from green. Using a machine straight stitch and referring to the photo on page 58 for placement, sew the rickrack vines to the quilt center, allowing the ends to extend past the raw edges of the quilt (the ends will be caught in the seam allowances when the gold border is added). Trim the vine ends even with the quilt edges.

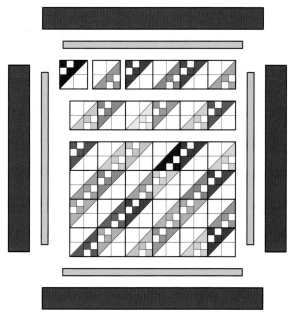

Assembly diagram

❸ Stitch gold strips to the quilt sides; trim even with the top and bottom. Stitch the remaining gold strips to the top and bottom; trim even with sides. Sew blue daisy strips to the sides; trim even. Sew the remaining blue daisy strips to the top and bottom; trim even.

❹ Using the vines and seams as a placement guide and referring to the photo, position the leaves and appliqué in place.

Quilting and Finishing

Layer, baste, and quilt. Mary machine quilted swirls and feathers on the quilt center and detail stitched the leaves. The gold border features a repeating leaf motif and the blue border is filled with a leafy vine. Bind the quilt with the blue daisy print.

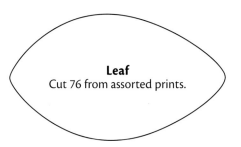

Leaf
Cut 76 from assorted prints.

Starring Repros!

EACH OF THESE CHEERFUL STAR BLOCKS features three different fabrics, one for the corner triangles, one for the star points, and one for the center triangles. It's up to you how much planning goes into your fabric combinations—the random look of the featured quilt, combined with the 1940s-inspired prints, gives it lots of vintage charm.

Finished quilt size: $72\frac{1}{2}$" x $84\frac{1}{2}$"
Number of blocks and finished size:
30 Star blocks, 12" x 12"

Fabric Requirements

- Cream solid fabric (block backgrounds), $3\frac{1}{2}$ yards

- Assorted prints (blocks, pieced border, pieced binding), 28 to 30 fat quarters* total

- Backing (piece lengthwise), $5\frac{1}{4}$ yards

- Batting, Full size

A fat quarter is an 18" x 20" to 22" cut of fabric or a true quarter of a yard.

Cutting Instructions

Cream solid fabric:
60 squares, $3\frac{7}{8}$" x $3\frac{7}{8}$"
120 rectangles, $3\frac{1}{2}$" x $6\frac{1}{2}$"
15 squares, $7\frac{1}{4}$" x $7\frac{1}{4}$"

Assorted prints:
Cut 30 sets of:
 2 matching squares, $3\frac{7}{8}$" x $3\frac{7}{8}$" (60 total)
 8 matching squares, $3\frac{1}{2}$" x $3\frac{1}{2}$" (240 total)
Cut a total of:
 15 squares, $7\frac{1}{4}$" x $7\frac{1}{4}$"
 66 rectangles, $4\frac{1}{2}$" x $6\frac{1}{2}$"
 4 squares, $6\frac{1}{2}$" x $6\frac{1}{2}$"
 22 strips, $2\frac{1}{2}$" x 18" (for binding)

Piecing the Blocks

❶ Draw a diagonal line on the wrong side of a cream $3\frac{7}{8}$" square. Place the marked square on an assorted $3\frac{7}{8}$" square, right sides together. Sew $\frac{1}{4}$" from each side of the marked line; cut apart on the marked line. Press open to make two pieced squares. Make 30 sets of four matching squares.

Make 30 sets
of 4 matching squares.

❷ Draw a diagonal line on the wrong side of an assorted $3\frac{1}{2}$" square. Place the marked square on a cream $3\frac{1}{2}$" x $6\frac{1}{2}$" rectangle, right sides together and aligning the raw edges. Sew on the marked line; trim away and discard the excess fabric. Press open. Repeat on the opposite end of the rectangle with a matching $3\frac{1}{2}$" square to make a pieced rectangle. Make 30 sets of four matching rectangles.

Make 30 sets
of 4 matching rectangles.

Guests will enjoy spending the night under this spectacular stellar display.
Designed by Dolores Smith and Sarah Maxwell. Machine quilted by Connie Gresham.

3 Draw two diagonal lines on the wrong side of a cream 7¼" square. Place the marked square on an assorted square, right sides together. Sew ¼" from each side of one line. Cutting on the line without stitching first, cut the sewn square into quarters. Press open to make four pieced triangles. Make 15 sets of four.

4 Stitch two matching pieced triangles from step 3 together to make a block center. Make 30 total.

Make 30 total.

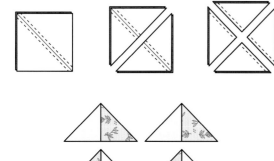

Make 15 sets of 4.

⑤ Sew three rows using four matching pieced squares, four matching pieced rectangles, and a block center. Sew the rows together to make a Star block. Make 30 total.

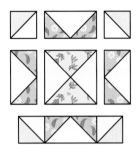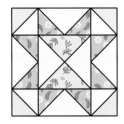

Make 30 total.

Quilt-Top Assembly

Refer to the assembly diagram for the following steps.

❶ Sew six rows of five blocks each. The blocks were rotated randomly in the featured quilt; do likewise if you wish. Sew the rows together.

❷ Sew 18 assorted 4½" x 6½" rectangles together along their long sides to make a side border. Make two total. Sew to the sides of the quilt center. Sew two strips of 15 rectangles each for the top and bottom borders. Sew 6½" squares to the ends of both strips and stitch to the top and bottom of the quilt.

Quilting and Finishing

❶ Layer, baste, and quilt. Connie machine quilted an overall flowers-and-swirls design.

❷ Sew the 22 assorted 2½" x 18" strips together end to end using diagonal seams. Bind the quilt with the pieced strip.

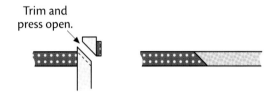

Trim and press open.

Assembly diagram

Fun A'Fair

CRAYON-COLORED TEXTURES, STRIPES, AND PRINTS all give this quilt lots of bright appeal. The large Pinwheel blocks start with strip-pieced squares for a contemporary spin.

Finished quilt size: 50½" x 64"

Number of blocks and finished size: 12 large Pinwheel blocks, 12" x 12"; 4 small Pinwheel blocks, 4" x 4"

Fabric Requirements

- Light yellow print and dark gold print (large blocks), 2 fat quarters* each

- Orange striped fabric and blue striped fabric (blocks, sashing posts), 1 fat quarter each

- Red print, purple-and-teal print, pink-and-gold print, purple print, and red-on-red print (large blocks, sashing), 1 fat quarter* each

- Teal print (large blocks, border, binding), 2½ yards

- Yellow-and-gold polka-dot fabric (small blocks), 1 fat quarter*

- Purple-on-purple print and orange-and-red print (sashing), 1 fat quarter* each

- Backing (piece widthwise), 3⅜ yards

- Batting, Twin size

- 6½" square acrylic ruler with 45° diagonal line

A fat quarter is an 18" x 20" to 22" cut of fabric or a true quarter of a yard.

Cutting Instructions

Light yellow print and dark gold print—cut from each:
12 strips, 3" x 18" (24 total)

Orange striped fabric—refer to the diagram top right to cut:
6 strips, 2" x 18"
4 squares, 2⅞" x 2⅞"
6 squares, 2" x 2"

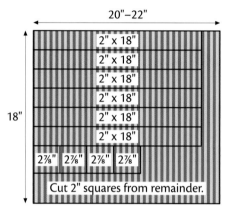

Stripe cutting diagram

(diagram labels: 20"–22"; 18"; 2" x 18" (six); 2⅞" (four); Cut 2" squares from remainder.)

Blue striped fabric—refer to the diagram above to cut:
6 strips, 2" x 18"
4 squares, 2⅞" x 2⅞"
14 squares, 2" x 2"

Red print, purple-and-teal print, pink-and-gold print, purple print, and red-on-red print—cut from each:
4 squares, 7" x 7" (20 total)
2 strips, 2" x 12½" (10 total)

Teal print:
*4 strips, 4½" x 60", cut on the lengthwise grain
4 squares, 7" x 7"
6 strips, 2½" x 42"

Yellow-and-gold polka-dot fabric:
8 squares, 2⅞" x 2⅞"

Purple-on-purple print:
10 strips, 2" x 12½"

Orange-and-red print:
11 strips, 2" x 12½"

*Cut first.

Set your stripes a-spinning in this fun pinwheel quilt designed by Colleen Reale and Chloe Anderson of Toadusew Creative Concepts. Machine quilted by Asta Dorsett.

Piecing the Blocks

❶ Sew light yellow and dark gold strips to the sides of an orange striped strip. Make 6. Press toward the orange striped strip. Cut 12 segments, 7" wide. In the same manner, make strip sets using the blue striped strips in the center and cut 12 segments, 7" wide.

7"

Make 6 strip sets.
Cut 12 segments.

7"

Make 6 strip sets.
Cut 12 segments.

❷ Draw a diagonal line on the wrong side of a red print 7" square. Place the marked square on an orange striped segment from step 1, right sides together. Sew ¼" from each side of the marked line; cut apart on the marked line. Press open to make pieced squares. Make eight total (half the pieced squares will have light yellow small triangles and half will have dark gold small triangles). In same manner, make pieced squares in the fabric combinations and quantities shown.

Make 8 total.

Make 8 total.   Make 8 total.   Make 8 total.

Make 8 total.   Make 8 total.

❸ Use a 6½" square acrylic ruler to trim a square to 6½", centering the rule on a pieced square and aligning the 45° diagonal line with the seam. Repeat for all pieced squares.

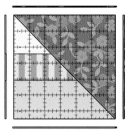

Center ruler and
trim to 6½" square.

❹ Use two assorted red or pink pieced squares with small gold triangles and two assorted purple or teal pieced squares with small gold triangles to make a Large Pinwheel block. Make six total. In the same manner, make six total with small light yellow triangles at the centers.

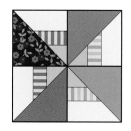

Make 6 total
with dark gold centers.

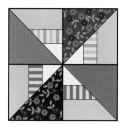

Make 6 total
with light yellow centers.

❺ Using the mark, stitch, cut, and press method from step 2, make small pieced squares in the fabric combinations and quantities shown.

Make 8.   Make 8.

❻ Sew two orange striped and two blue striped small pieced squares together to make a Small Pinwheel block. Make 4.

Make 4.

Quilt-Top Assembly

Refer to the assembly diagram for the following steps.

❶ Sew five sashing rows using four striped 2" squares and three 2" x 12½" sashing strips each. Note: Blue and purple squares and strips are placed on the outside edges of the quilt center; red, orange, and pink squares and strips are placed within the quilt center. Stitch four block rows using four sashing strips and three Large Pinwheel blocks each, alternating the placement of the blocks with dark gold and light yellow centers. Sew the rows together.

❷ Measure the exact width of the quilt center (from raw edge to raw edge). Trim two teal print strips to this measurement and sew small Pinwheel blocks to both ends, watching orientation. Stitch the untrimmed teal strips to the sides; trim even with the top and bottom. Sew the pieced strips to the top and bottom.

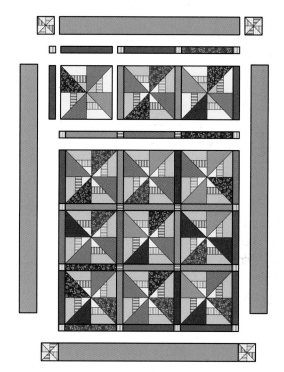

Assembly diagram

Quilting and Finishing

Layer, baste, and quilt. Asta machine quilted the blocks and border in the ditch. The large triangles in the large blocks and the yellow triangles of the border blocks are stitched with curved lines. The yellow and gold areas of the large blocks and the sashing posts are filled with swirls and the sashing strips feature adjoining circles. A repeating flower motif fills the border. Bind with teal print.

Independence Day

WE INSTRUCT YOU TO USE A QUICK MARK, SEW, AND TRIM METHOD for piecing the blocks. Although this method uses a bit more fabric than traditional piecing methods, we feel the increased accuracy is worth it. Enjoy creating a coordinating project with the leftover half-square triangles.

Finished quilt size: 60½" x 80½"
Number of blocks and finished size:
48 Independence blocks, 10" x 10"

Fabric Requirements

- Assorted blue prints (blocks), 5 to 6 yards *total*

- Assorted white prints (blocks), 5 to 6 yards *total*

- Assorted red prints (blocks, binding), 1¾ to 2 yards *total*

- Backing (piece lengthwise), 5 yards

- Batting, Twin size

Cutting Instructions

Assorted blue prints—cut *24 sets* of:
8 matching squares, 4¼" x 4¼" (192 total)
4 matching squares, 5½" x 5½" (96 total)

Assorted white prints—cut *24 sets* of:
8 matching squares, 4¼" x 4¼" (192 total)
4 matching squares, 5½" x 5½" (96 total)

Assorted red prints—cut a *total* of:
*8 strips, 2½" x 42"
384 squares, 1¾" x 1¾"

*Cut first.

Piecing the Blocks

❶ Draw a diagonal line on the wrong side of a blue 4¼" square with the marking tool of your choice. Place the blue square on a white 5½" square, right sides together and aligning the raw edges. Stitch on the drawn line; trim away and discard the excess fabric. Press open. Repeat the process on the opposite corner with a matching blue 4¼" square. Make 24 sets of four matching pieced squares. In the same manner, use white 4¼" squares on blue 5½" square to make pieced square as shown. Make 24 sets of four matching units.

Make 24 sets of 4 matching units.   Make 24 sets of 4 matching units.

A red-white-and-blue color scheme is a perennial favorite. Use your favorites for this punchy, patriotic quilt. Designed by Ann Weber.

❷ Repeat the marking, stitching, trimming, and pressing process on the corners of the pieced squares using the red 1¾" squares. Make 24 sets of four of each color arrangement.

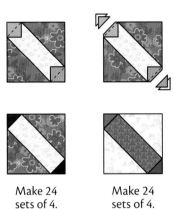

Make 24 sets of 4.   Make 24 sets of 4.

❸ Arrange and sew four matching pieced squares together to make an Independence block. Make 24 of each for 48 total.

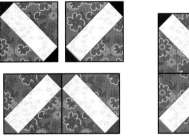
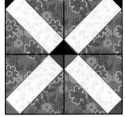

Make 24 total.

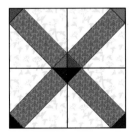

Make 24 total.

Quilt-Top Assembly

Arrange and stitch eight rows of six blocks each, alternating the blue and white blocks. Sew the rows together.

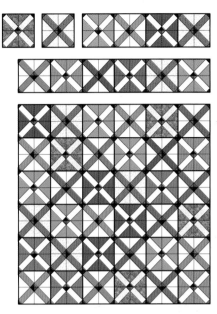

Assembly diagram

Quilting and Finishing

❶ Layer and baste the quilt top for the quilting method of your choice. The featured quilt was machine quilted. A gentle wave is centered along each diagonal strip. The pieced blue/white squares (formed at the block intersections) feature echo-quilted flower motifs.

❷ To make the pieced binding, cut the red 2½" x 42" strips in half, and then piece them together as shown. Bind the quilt with the pieced strip.

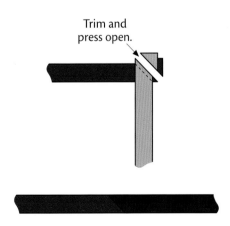

Trim and press open.

Crazy Geese

BE SURE TO INCLUDE A WIDE RANGE OF VALUES in your fabric selections, from medium/light to very dark for the reds and very light to medium for the tans, to add sparkle and interest to your version of this striking quilt. The red binding, pieced from assorted prints, is a perfect finishing touch. See the tip box below for more on using scraps.

Finished quilt size: 45½" x 54½"
Number of blocks and finished size:
90 Crazy Geese blocks, 3" x 9"

Fabric Requirements

- Assorted tan prints (blocks), 1¾ to 2¼ yards *total*

- Assorted red prints (blocks, binding), 2¼ to 2¾ yards *total*

- Backing (piece widthwise), 3 yards

- Batting, Twin size

Cutting Instructions

The piecing patterns are on page 75.

Assorted tan prints—cut a *total* of:
42 using pattern A
48 *each* using patterns B and B reversed (BR)

Assorted red prints—cut a *total* of:
48 using pattern A
42 *each* using patterns B and BR
6 strips, 2½" x 42"

Showcase Your Scraps

Ann and Joanne say, "We like to think of scrap quilts as 'best of fabrics' quilts! We chose at least 10 to 15 fabrics in each of the assorted groups (tans and reds) for this quilt, looking for a variety in both color and pattern. Here are the details of some of our selections."

Designed by Ann Weber and Joanne Rowicki.

Piecing the Blocks

Sew tan B and BR triangles to a red A triangle, aligning the match points. Make 48 total Crazy Geese blocks. In same manner, use red B and BR triangles and a tan A triangle to make Crazy Geese block. Make 42 total.

Make 48 total.

Make 42 total.

Quilt-Top Assembly

Sew 15 vertical rows of six blocks each, watching placement and orientation. Sew the rows together.

Quilting and Finishing

❶ Layer, baste, and quilt. The featured quilt was machine quilted in the ditch along the large zigzags. Two lines of straight quilting with red thread follow the zigzag pattern in the red patches and four lines of wavy stitching in cream thread follow the zigzag pattern in the cream patches.

❷ Sew red 42"-long strips together end to end using diagonal seams as shown. Bind with the pieced strip.

Trim and press open.

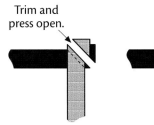

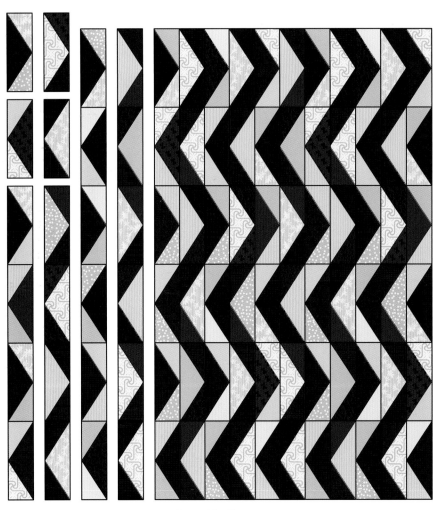

Assembly diagram

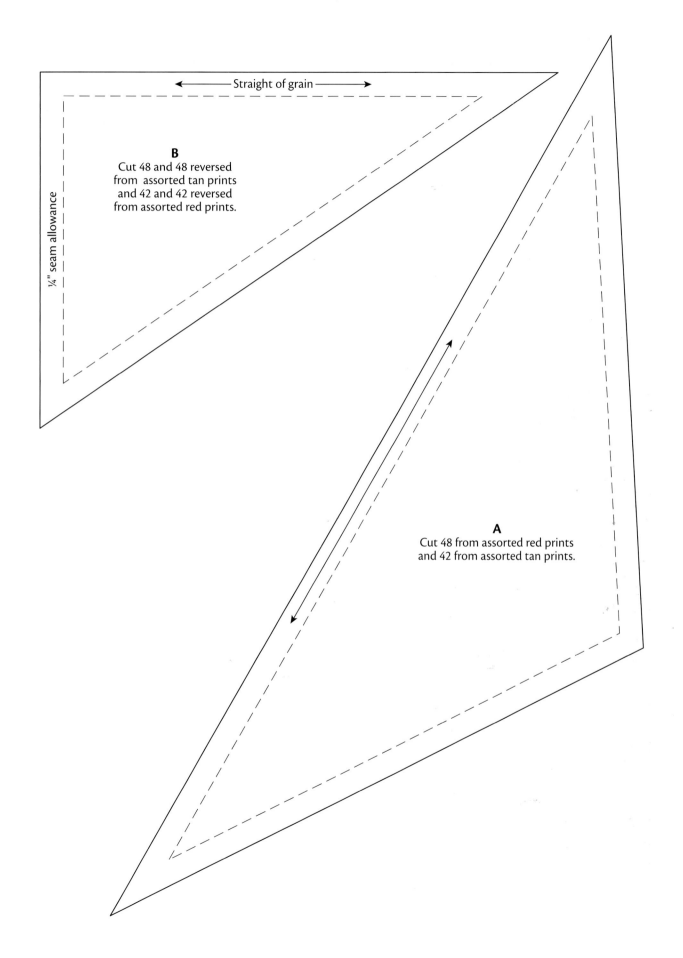

Straight of grain

¼" seam allowance

B
Cut 48 and 48 reversed
from assorted tan prints
and 42 and 42 reversed
from assorted red prints.

A
Cut 48 from assorted red prints
and 42 from assorted tan prints.

Nines and Vines

"I LOVE THE ILLUSION THAT I AM USING UP MY STASH when I make a scrap quilt!" Kathie says. "There's a challenge to using multiple fabrics in one quilt, and using 50 fabrics is lots more fun than using 5. I made these Double Nine Patch blocks with fabrics I liked, adding in colors that enhanced previous choices as the quilt grew."

Finished quilt size: 55½" x 73½"
Number of blocks and finished size:
24 Double Nine Patch blocks, 9" x 9"

Fabric Requirements

- Assorted medium or dark prints (blocks, flowers), 2½ to 3 yards *total*

- Assorted cream prints (blocks), 2½ to 3 yards *total*

- Green-and-red print (inner border, outer border corners), ¾ yard

- Beige print (outer border), 1¾ yards

- Brown print (vine), ⅝ yard

- Assorted green prints (leaves), ¼ yard *total*

- Red print (binding), ⅝ yard

- Backing (piece widthwise), 3⅝ yards

- Batting, Twin size

- Bias bar, ½" (optional)

Cutting Instructions

The appliqué patterns, printed without a seam allowance for paper-backed fusible web, are on page 81.

Assorted medium or dark prints:
Cut 24 matching sets of:
   2 strips, 1½" x 18" (48 total)
   1 strip, 1½" x 10" (24 total)

Cut a total of:
   24 using pattern A
   24 using pattern B

Assorted cream prints:
Cut 12 matching sets of:
   1 strip, 1½" x 18" (12 total)
   2 strips, 1½" x 10" (24 total)
   4 squares, 3½" x 3½" (48 total)
Cut 12 matching sets of:
   1 strip, 1½" x 18" (12 total)
   2 strips, 1½" x 10" (24 total)
   5 squares, 3½" x 3½" (60 total)

Green-and-red print:
2 strips, 2" x 58", pieced from 3 strips, 42" long
2 strips, 2" x 44", pieced from 3 strips, 42" long
4 squares, 8½" x 8½"

Beige print:
2 strips, 8½" x 62", cut on the lengthwise grain
2 strips, 8½" x 44", cut on the lengthwise grain

Brown print:
1 bias-cut strip, 1½" x 175", cut from an 18" square*

Assorted green prints—cut a *total* of:
12 using pattern C

Red print:
7 strips, 2½" x 42"

Instructions for how to make continuous bias from a square are on page 95.

Create classic country appeal with Kathie Holland's Double Nine Patch quilt
embellished with an appliqué border.

Piecing the Blocks

❶ Sew matching assorted medium or dark print 1½" x 18" strips to the sides of a cream print 1½" x 18" strip. Make 24 total. Press the seam allowances as shown. Cut segments, 1½" wide, in the quantities shown.

1½"

Make 24 strip sets.
Cut 10 segments each from 12 strip sets.
Cut 8 segments each from remaining 12 strip sets.

❷ Repeat the process using two matching cream print strips and a medium or dark 1½" x 10" strip. Make 24 total. Press and cut segments, 1½" wide, in the quantities shown.

1½"

Make 24 strip sets.
Cut 5 segments each from 12 strip sets.
Cut 4 segments each from remaining 12 strip sets.

❸ Sew the segments together to make nine-patch units. Make 12 sets of five matching and 12 sets of four matching units.

Make 12 sets
of 5 matching and
12 sets of 4 matching units.

❹ Sew three rows using five matching nine-patch units and four matching cream 3½" squares. Sew the rows together to make a Double Nine Patch block. Make 12 total. In the same manner, make 12 blocks using five matching cream squares and four matching nine-patch squares each.

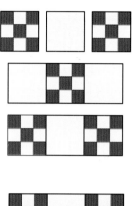

Make 12 total.

Make 12 total.

Quilt-Top Assembly and Appliqué

Refer to the assembly diagram for the following steps.

❶ Sew six rows of four blocks each, alternating the blocks as shown. Sew the rows together. Sew the green-and-red 58"-long strips to the sides; trim even with the top and bottom. Sew the remaining green-and-red strips to the top and bottom; trim even with the sides.

❷ Measure the exact width of the quilt center (from raw edge to raw edge). Trim the beige 44"-long strips to this measurement and sew the green-and-red 8½" squares to both ends. Stitch the beige 62"-long strips to sides of the quilt; trim even. Sew the pieced strips to the top and bottom.

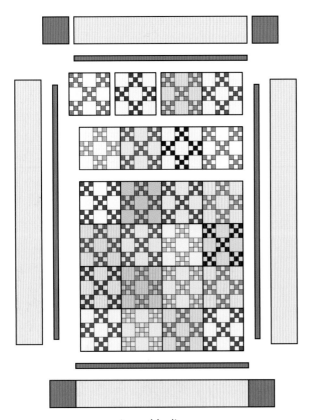

Assembly diagram

❸ To make vine, fold the brown print bias-cut 1½" x 175" strip in half, wrong sides together. Stitch ¼" from the raw edges. Trim the seam allowance to ⅛". Press the tube flat, centering the seam allowance on the back so the raw edge isn't visible from the front. Using a ½" bias bar makes pressing faster and easier. Cut the strip into two lengths, 33" each, and two lengths, 53" each.

❹ Referring to the photo on page 78, position the 33"-long vines on the top and bottom borders and the 53"-long vines on the side borders. Appliqué in place. Position the A, B, and C shapes on the fabric; appliqué in place.

Quilting and Finishing

Layer, baste, and quilt. Kathie machine quilted diagonal lines intersecting the 3½" squares. She quilted the appliqué shapes in the ditch and filled the background and corner squares with meandering lines. A wavy line runs the length of each inner-border strip. Bind with red print.

Recreating the Look

Choosing a different assorted medium/dark print and cream print pairing to use in each block will give your version of this quilt the classic country appeal of the original. Short strip sets speed construction without sacrificing scrappy style. Note that Kathie cut her stars casually, with some larger and some smaller than our pattern. Do likewise if you wish.

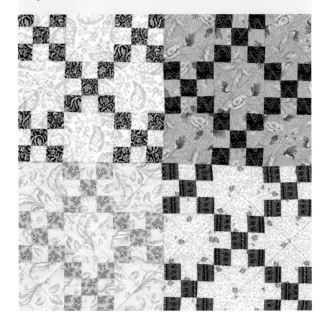

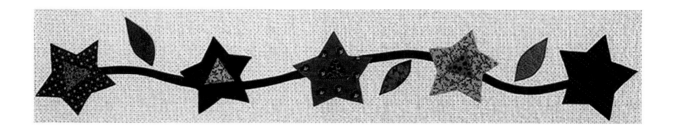

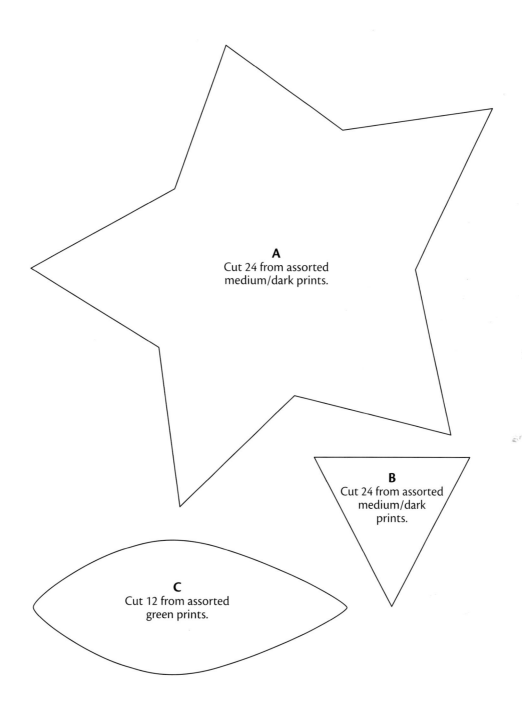

A
Cut 24 from assorted
medium/dark prints.

B
Cut 24 from assorted
medium/dark
prints.

C
Cut 12 from assorted
green prints.

Tropical Fruits

STRIKING AND SIMPLE, THIS QUILT MADE OF BATIKS GLOWS LIKE A SUMMER GARDEN. Medium and dark batiks in a rainbow of assorted colors from pink to dark blue provide the sparkle; turquoise fabrics add a sense of peace. Notice that Sarah and Dolores picked turquoise batiks that are similar to one another, but have slight differences in color or texture. This gives the quilt a cohesive, rich look.

Finished quilt size: $63\frac{3}{4}$" x $76\frac{7}{8}$"

Number of blocks and finished size: 72 Nine Patch blocks, 6" x 6"; 30 Framed Square blocks, 6" x 6"

Fabric Requirements

- Assorted medium and dark batiks (blocks), $2\frac{3}{4}$ to $3\frac{1}{4}$ yards *total*

- Assorted turquoise batiks (blocks, setting squares and triangles), $2\frac{1}{8}$ to $2\frac{1}{2}$ yards *total*

- Assorted blue and purple batiks (blocks), 1 to $1\frac{1}{4}$ yards *total*

- Turquoise print batik (blocks, setting squares and triangles, binding), $1\frac{3}{8}$ yards

- Backing (piece lengthwise), $4\frac{7}{8}$ yards

- Batting, Twin size

Cutting Instructions

Assorted medium and dark batiks:

Cut 72 sets of:

    5 matching squares, $2\frac{1}{2}$" x $2\frac{1}{2}$" (360 total)

Cut 30 matching sets of:

    2 squares, $2\frac{1}{2}$" x $2\frac{1}{2}$" (60 total)

    2 strips, $2\frac{1}{2}$" x $6\frac{1}{2}$" (60 total)

Assorted turquoise batiks:

Cut 28 sets of:

    4 matching squares, $2\frac{1}{2}$" x $2\frac{1}{2}$" (112 total)

Cut a total of:

    *6 squares, 11" x 11"; cut into quarters diagonally to make 24 triangles (2 left over)

    8 squares, $2\frac{1}{2}$" x $2\frac{1}{2}$"

    21 squares, $6\frac{1}{2}$" x $6\frac{1}{2}$"

    2 squares, 6" x 6"; cut in half diagonally to make 4 triangles

Assorted blue and purple batiks:

Cut 40 sets of:

    4 matching squares, $2\frac{1}{2}$" x $2\frac{1}{2}$" (160 total)

Cut a total of:

    22 squares, $2\frac{1}{2}$" x $2\frac{1}{2}$"

Turquoise print batik:

*2 squares, 11" x 11"; cut into quarters diagonally to make 8 triangles

*5 squares, $6\frac{1}{2}$" x $6\frac{1}{2}$"

16 squares, $2\frac{1}{2}$" x $2\frac{1}{2}$"

8 strips, $2\frac{1}{2}$" x 42"

*Cut first.

Easy blocks form a riot of color in this quilt designed by Sarah Maxwell and Delores Smith. Machine quilted by Connie Gresham

❸ The setting triangles on all edges and corners are cut oversized so the quilt edges can be trimmed even after assembly. Sew 16 diagonal rows using the assorted turquoise and turquoise print 11" triangles, the blocks, and the $6\frac{1}{2}$" squares, watching the placement carefully. Sew the rows together. Stitch the assorted turquoise $6\frac{1}{2}$" triangles to the corners. Trim the edges even.

Assembly diagram

Quilt-Top Assembly

❶ Stitch together one set of five matching medium or dark $2\frac{1}{2}$" squares and one set of four matching turquoise, blue or purple, or turquoise print $2\frac{1}{2}$" squares to make a Nine Patch block. Make 72 total.

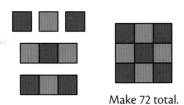

Make 72 total.

Quilting and Finishing

Layer, baste, and quilt. Connie machine quilted an overall curlicue pattern. Bind with the turquoise print batik.

❷ Sew one matching set of two assorted $2\frac{1}{2}$" squares and two assorted $2\frac{1}{2}$" x $6\frac{1}{2}$" strips to one assorted turquoise or assorted blue or purple $2\frac{1}{2}$" square to make a Framed Square block. Make 30 total.

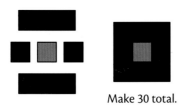

Make 30 total.

Let's Celebrate!

With easy piecing and fast fusible appliqué, you can have this quilt ready for your next family birthday celebration. Children and adults alike will love this cheerful, festive quilt.

Every day's a party when this festive quilt, designed by Heidi Pridemore, is on the scene.

Finished quilt size: 41½" x 44½"
Number of blocks and finished size:
6 Pinwheel blocks, 5" x 5"

Fabric Requirements

- Yellow print (blocks, balloons), ½ yard
- Lavender print (blocks), ¼ yard
- Blue balloon print (setting squares), ½ yard
- Pink print (setting strips, balloons, binding), ¾ yard
- Polka-dot print (appliqué background strips), 1⅛ yards
- Green print and blue print (balloons), 1 fat eighth* *each*
- White solid fabric (balloon highlights), 3" x 17" piece
- Multicolored diagonal-striped fabric (inner border), ⅜ yard
- Lavender cake print (outer border), ¾ yard
- ⅛"-wide paper-backed fusible web, 1 yard
- ⅛"-wide assorted colors of ribbon, 3 yards *total*
- Backing (piece widthwise), 2⅞ yards
- Batting, Twin size

*A fat eighth is a 9" x 20" to 22" cut of fabric.

Cutting Instructions

Appliqué patterns, printed without a seam allowance for paper-backed fusible web, are on page 89.

Yellow print and lavender print—cut from *each*:
12 squares, 3⅜" x 3⅜" (24 total)

Blue balloon print:
8 squares, 5½" x 5½"

Pink print:
4 strips, 1½" x 35½"
4 strips, 2½" x 42"

Polka-dot print:
3 strips, 6½" x 35½"

Multicolored diagonal-striped fabric:
2 strips, 1½" x 42"
2 strips, 1½" x 45", pieced from 3 strips, 42" long

Lavender cake print:
2 strips, 4" x 42"
2 strips, 4" x 45", pieced from 3 strips, 42" long

Quilt-Top Assembly

❶ Draw a diagonal line on the wrong side of a yellow square. Place the marked square on a lavender square, right sides together. Sew a ¼" on each side of the marked line; cut apart on the marked line. Press open to make two pieced squares. Repeat to make 24.

Make 24.

❷ Sew four pieced squares together to make a Pinwheel block; make 6.

Make 6.

❸ Sew two strips of four blue balloon print squares and three Pinwheel blocks each, alternating the squares and blocks as shown. Stitch pink 35½"-long strips to each side of the Pinwheel block strips. Sew the three polka-dot print 6½" x 35½" strips and the Pinwheel block strips together as shown.

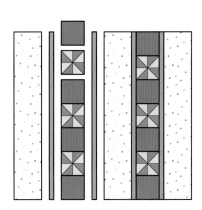

❹ Trace patterns A and B on the paper side of paper-backed fusible web. Cut apart, leaving a small margin beyond the drawn lines. Following the manufacturer's instructions, fuse to the wrong side of the appropriate fabrics; cut apart on the drawn lines. You will need 12 of each appliqué shape.

❺ Using the seam lines as a placement guide, position and fuse the appliqué shapes on the polka-dot strips. Use a machine buttonhole stitch around the edges of the shapes.

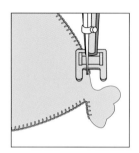

❻ Cut ⅛"-wide assorted ribbon into varying lengths from 3" to 8" each. Position ribbon balloon strings so they appear to be tied to the base of each balloon and are trailing below the balloons (the three lower balloon strings are caught in the border seam). When you're pleased with the arrangement, pin and sew down the center of each ribbon. Note: Heidi used fusible ribbon, called Hot Ribbon Art by Junko, to make positioning easier.

❼ Sew a 42"-long multicolored diagonal-striped strip and a 42"-long lavender cake strip together. Make two and stitch to the sides of the quilt center. Trim even with the top and bottom. Stitch 45"-long striped and lavender strips together; make 2. Sew to the top and bottom of the quilt; trim even with the sides.

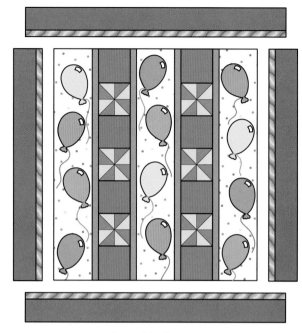

Assembly diagram

Quilting and Finishing

Layer, baste, and quilt. Heidi machine quilted in the ditch along the seams and appliqué. Bind the quilt with the pink print strips.

Bright and Bold

This bright version of the quilt has a more masculine feel than the version shown on page 86.

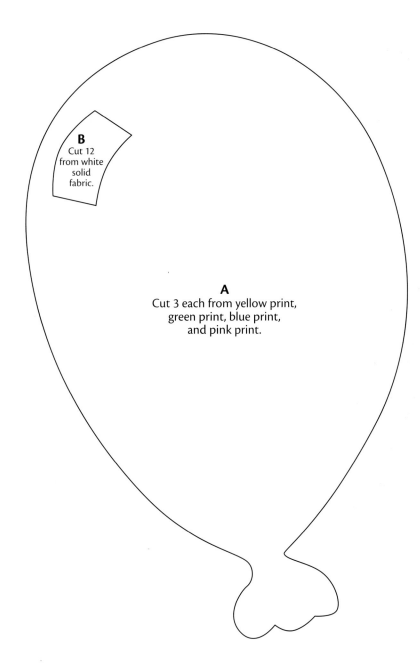

B
Cut 12
from white
solid
fabric.

A
Cut 3 each from yellow print,
green print, blue print,
and pink print.

Basic Quiltmaking Instructions

Rotary Cutting

For those unfamiliar with rotary cutting, a brief introduction is provided below.

❶ To prepare the fabric, iron it to remove wrinkles. Fold the fabric and match selvages, aligning the crosswise and lengthwise grains as much as possible. Place the folded fabric on the cutting mat with the folded edge closest to you.

❷ Align a square ruler along the folded edge of the fabric. Then place a long, straight ruler to the left of the square ruler, just covering the uneven raw edges of the left side of the fabric. Remove the square ruler and cut along the right edge of the long ruler, rolling the rotary cutter away from you. Discard this strip. (Reverse this procedure if you are left-handed.)

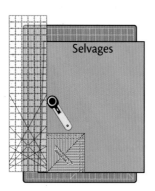

Selvages

❸ To cut strips, align the required measurement on the ruler with the newly cut edge of the fabric. For example, to cut a 3"-wide strip, place the 3" ruler mark on the edge of the fabric.

❹ To cut squares or rectangles, cut strips in the required widths. Trim away the selvage ends. Align the required measurement on the ruler with the left edge of the strip and cut a square or rectangle.

❺ For half-square triangles, cut squares in half diagonally. For quarter-square triangles, cut squares into quarters diagonally.

Two half-square triangles cut from one square

Four quarter-square triangles cut from one square

Cutting Bias Strips

❶ Position the fabric on the grid side of the cutting mat so that the lengthwise and crosswise grains of the fabric align with the vertical and horizontal grid lines.

❷ Begin cutting approximately 6" from the lower-left corner of the fabric. Align the 45° line on the ruler with the first horizontal grid line visible on the mat below the fabric's bottom edge. Make a cut, creating a waste triangle.

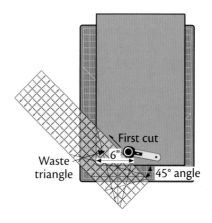

First cut

6"

Waste triangle

45° angle

❸ Align the required measurement on your ruler with the newly cut edge and cut the first strip.

❹ Continue cutting until you have the number of strips required. Periodically recheck the position of the 45° angle marking on the ruler. If necessary, re-trim the cut edge of the fabric to "true up" the angle.

Machine Piecing

The most important thing to remember about machine piecing is to maintain a consistent $1/4$"-wide seam allowance. This is necessary for seams to match and for the resulting block or quilt to measure the desired finished size. Measurements for all components of each quilt are based on blocks that finish accurately to the desired size plus $1/4$" on each edge for seam allowances.

Take the time to establish an exact $1/4$"-wide seam guide on your machine. Some machines have a special quilting foot that measures exactly $1/4$" from the center needle position to the edge of the foot. If your machine doesn't have such a foot, create a seam guide by placing the edge of a piece of tape or moleskin $1/4$" away from the needle.

Chain Piecing

Chain piecing saves time and thread. It's helpful when you're sewing many identical units. Simply sew the first pair of pieces from cut edge to cut edge. At the end of the seam, stop sewing, but do not cut the thread. Feed the next pair of pieces under the presser foot, as close as possible to the first. Continue sewing without cutting threads. When all the pieces are sewn, remove the chain from the machine, clip the threads, and press.

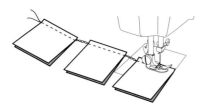

Appliqué

There are many techniques for appliqué and there's not space to cover all of them here. For additional information on other methods or more details, consult some of the many excellent books on the topic, or visit your local quilt shop to look into classes.

Making Templates

To make permanent plastic templates, place template plastic over each pattern piece and trace with a fine-line permanent marker. Do not add seam allowances. Cut out the templates on the drawn lines. Mark the pattern name and piece number (if applicable) on the templates.

Hand Appliqué

❶ Place the template right side up on the right side of the fabric and trace around it. Cut out each fabric piece, leaving a scant $1/4$" seam allowance around each tracing. Turn under the seam allowance and finger-press. Clip the seam allowance as necessary. Baste close to the edge to hold the seam allowance in place. Do not turn under edges that will be covered by another piece.

❷ Pin the pieces in place on the background fabric, noting where one piece may overlap another. A seam allowance that is overlapped by another piece need not be basted under.

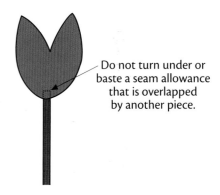

Do not turn under or baste a seam allowance that is overlapped by another piece.

❸ Use the traditional appliqué stitch described on page 92 to sew your appliqué pieces to the background.

Freezer Paper for Hand or Machine Appliqué

This method of preparing appliqué shapes can be used for both hand appliqué and machine appliqué.

❶ Trace the appliqué pattern onto the dull side of freezer paper. Trace the pattern in reverse if it is asymmetrical and has not already been reversed for tracing. For symmetrical patterns, it does not matter.

❷ Cut the freezer-paper template on the drawn lines and press it to the wrong side of the appliqué fabric.

❸ Cut out the fabric shapes, adding a scant ¼" seam allowance around each shape.

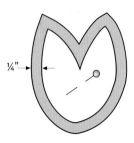

❹ Turn the seam allowance over the edge of the paper and baste it to the paper. Clip the corners and baste inner curves first. On outer curves, take small running stitches through the fabric only, to ease in fullness.

❺ For sharp points, first fold the corner to the inside; then fold the remaining seam allowances over the paper.

Fold corners to inside.　　Fold remaining seam allowances over paper.

❻ When all seam allowances are turned and basted, press the appliqués.

❼ Pin and stitch the pieces to the background by hand or machine.

❽ After stitching, remove the basting stitches, carefully slit the background fabric behind the appliqué shape, and pull out the paper. Use tweezers if necessary to loosen the freezer paper.

Freezer Paper for Hand Appliqué

You can use freezer paper either on top or underneath as a guide for turning under seam allowances when doing hand appliqué using the traditional appliqué stitch. You can reuse the templates several times before discarding them.

Freezer Paper on Top. Trace the appliqué pattern (not reversed) onto the dull side of freezer paper and cut on the drawn lines. Press to the right side of the chosen fabric and cut out the shape, adding a scant ¼"-wide seam allowance all around. Pin the piece to the background, paper side up, and use the edge of the paper as a guide for turning under

the seam allowance as you stitch. Remove the paper when you are done stitching.

Freezer Paper Underneath. Follow steps 1 through 3 of "Freezer Paper for Hand or Machine Appliqué" above. Pin the piece to the background, paper side down, and use the edge of the freezer paper as a guide for turning under the seam allowance as you stitch. Remove the paper with tweezers when you are about ½" from where you started stitching.

Needle-Turn Hand Appliqué

Use a longer needle, a Sharp or milliner's needle, to help you control the seam allowance and turn it under as you stitch.

❶ Place the template right side up on the right side of the fabric and trace around it with a No. 2 pencil or a white pencil, depending on your fabric color and print.

❷ Cut the shape out, adding a scant ¼" seam allowance all around.

❸ Pin or baste the appliqué piece in position on the background fabric.

❹ Beginning on a straight edge, bring your needle up through the background and the appliqué piece, just inside the drawn line. Use the tip of the needle to gently turn under the seam allowance, about ½" at a time. Hold the turned seam allowance firmly between the thumb and first finger of one hand as you stitch the appliqué to the background fabric with your other hand. Use the traditional appliqué stitch described below.

Traditional Appliqué Stitch

❶ Thread a needle with a single strand of thread and knot one end. Use a thread color that matches the appliqué piece.

❷ Slip the needle into the seam allowance from the wrong side of the appliqué, bringing it out on the fold line. Start the first stitch by inserting the needle into the background fabric right next to the folded edge of the appliqué where the thread exits the appliqué shape.

❸ Let the needle travel under the background fabric, parallel to the edge of the appliqué; bring the needle up about ⅛" away through the edge of the appliqué, catching only one or two threads of the folded edge. Insert the needle into the background fabric right next to the folded edge. Let the needle travel under the background, and again, bring it up about ⅛" away, catching just the edge of the appliqué. Give the thread a slight tug and continue stitching.

Appliqué stitch

❹ Stitch around the appliqué, taking a couple of stitches beyond where you started. Knot the thread on the wrong side of the background fabric, behind the appliqué.

Fusible Appliqué

This appliqué method is fast and easy. Many fusing products are available for applying one piece of fabric to another, but fabrics do stiffen after application, so choose a lightweight fusible web. Follow the manufacturer's directions for the product you select. Unless the patterns are symmetrical or the pattern has already been reversed, you must *reverse the templates when you draw them onto the paper side of the fusible web.* Do not add seam allowances to the appliqué pieces, but leave a ¼" to ½" cutting margin around each shape drawn on the fusible appliqué. For large appliqués, you can cut out the center of the fusible web, leaving a "donut" of web so that the centers of your appliqués will remain soft and unfused.

For quilts that will be washed often, finish the edges of the appliqués by stitching around them with a decorative stitch, such as a blanket stitch (by hand or machine) or zigzag stitch.

Machine Appliqué

For the most "invisible" stitches, use monofilament thread—clear for light-colored appliqués or smoke for medium or dark colors. If you want your stitches to show as a more decorative element, use a matching or contrasting-color thread in the top of your machine. Use a

neutral-color thread to match your background fabric in the bobbin.

❶ Set your machine for a small zigzag stitch (about ¹⁄₁₆" wide) and do a practice sample to test your stitches and tension. An open-toe presser foot is helpful for machine appliqué.

❷ Begin stitching with the needle just outside the appliqué piece and take two or three straight stitches in place first to lock the thread. Make sure the needle is on the right of the appliqué and that the zigzag stitches will go into the appliqué piece. (You can use any decorative stitch on your machine.)

❸ Stitch curved shapes slowly to maintain control, stopping and pivoting as needed.

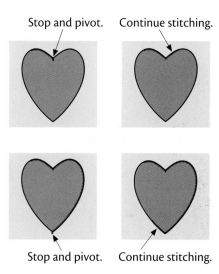

Stop and pivot.   Continue stitching.

Stop and pivot.   Continue stitching.

❹ Stitch completely around the appliqué until you are slightly beyond the starting point. Take two or three straight stitches in place to lock the thread and clip the thread tails.

❺ To remove freezer paper, carefully trim away the background fabric behind the appliqué, leaving a generous ¼" seam allowance to keep your appliqué secure. Use tweezers as needed. (Bias stems and vines and fused appliqué shapes will not have paper to remove, so it's not necessary to cut away the background.)

Borders

For best results, measure the quilt top before cutting and sewing border strips to the quilt. Measure the quilt top through the center in both directions to determine how long to cut the border strips. This step ensures that the finished quilt will be as straight and as "square" as possible, without wavy edges.

Many of these quilts call for plain border strips. Some of these strips are cut along the crosswise grain and joined where extra length is needed. Others are cut lengthwise and do not need to be pieced.

❶ Measure the length of the quilt top through the center. Cut two borders to this measurement. Determine the midpoints of the border and quilt top by folding them in half and creasing or pinning the centers. Then pin the borders to opposite sides of the quilt top, matching the center marks and ends and easing as necessary. Sew the border strips in place. Press the seam allowances toward the borders.

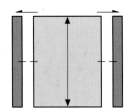

Measure center of quilt,
top to bottom. Mark centers.

❷ Measure the width of the quilt top through the center, including the side borders just added. Cut two borders to this measurement. Mark the centers of the quilt edges and the border strips. Pin the borders to the top and bottom edges of the quilt top, matching the center marks and ends and easing as necessary. Sew the border strips in place. Press the seam allowances toward the borders.

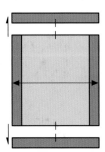

Measure center of quilt, side to side,
including border strips. Mark centers.

Finishing

The quilt "sandwich" consists of backing, batting, and the quilt top. Cut the quilt backing 4" to 6" longer and wider than the quilt top. Baste together with thread for hand quilting or safety pins for machine quilting. Quilt by hand or machine.

Hand Quilting

To quilt by hand, you will need short, sturdy needles (called Betweens), quilting thread, and a thimble to fit the middle finger of your sewing hand. Most quilters also use a frame or hoop to support their work.

❶ Thread a needle with a single strand of quilting thread, knot one end, and insert the needle in the top layer about 1" from the place where you want to start stitching. Pull the needle out at the point where quilting will begin and gently pull the thread until the knot pops through the fabric and into the batting.

❷ Take small, evenly spaced stitches through all three quilt layers. Rock the needle up and down through all layers until you have three or four stitches on the needle. Place your other hand under the quilt so that you can feel the needle point with the tip of your finger when a stitch is taken.

❸ To end a line of quilting, make a small knot close to the last stitch; then backstitch, running the thread a needle's length through the batting. Gently pull the thread until the knot pops into the batting; clip the thread at the quilt's surface.

Machine Quilting

For straight-line quilting, it's extremely helpful to have a walking foot to help feed the quilt layers through the machine without shifting or puckering. Some machines have a built-in walking foot; other machines require a separate attachment. Read the machine's instruction manual for special tension settings to sew through extra fabric thicknesses.

For curved designs or stippling, use a darning foot and lower the feed dogs for free-motion quilting. Free-motion quilting allows the fabric to move freely under the foot of the sewing machine. Because the feed dogs are lowered, the stitch length is determined by the speed at which you run the machine and feed the fabric under the foot. Practice on scraps until you get the feel of controlling the motion of the fabric with your hands.

Cutting Continuous Bias Strips from a Square

❶ Remove the selvages from the fabric and cut a square as directed in the project instructions. (A 40" square should make about 16 yards of 2½"-wide bias strip.)

❷ Lightly label the square as shown. Cut the square in half diagonally to make triangles.

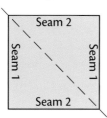

❸ With right sides together and raw edges aligned, join the triangles (seam 1) to form a parallelogram. Press the seam allowances open. Measure and mark across the parallelogram with lines equal to the width of your bias strip as shown.

 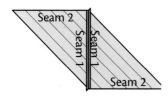

❹ Form a tube by aligning the edges marked *seam 2,* matching your marked lines and offsetting the edge one strip width beyond the line. Stitch and press the seam allowances open.

❺ Starting at the offset end, cut around the tube on the marked lines to make a continuous bias strip.

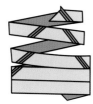

Binding

The quilt directions tell you how wide to cut the strips for binding. Bindings are generally cut anywhere from 2" to 2½" wide, depending on personal preference. You will need enough strips to go around the perimeter of the quilt plus 12".

❶ Sew the strips together end to end to make one long piece of binding. Join the strips at right angles and stitch from corner to corner. Trim the excess fabric and press the seam allowances open.

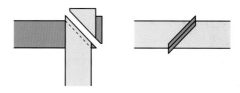

❷ Trim one end of the binding strip at a 45° angle. Turn under ¼" and press.

❸ Fold the strip in half lengthwise, wrong sides together, and press.

❹ Trim the batting and backing even with the quilt top.

❺ Starting in the middle of one side and using a ¼"-wide seam allowance, stitch the binding to the quilt. Keep the raw edges even with the quilt-top edge. Begin stitching 1" to 2" from the start of the binding. End the stitching ¼" from the corner of the quilt and backstitch. Clip the thread.

❻ Turn the quilt so that you will be stitching along the next side. Fold the binding up, away from the quilt; then fold it back down onto itself, even with the raw edge of the quilt top.

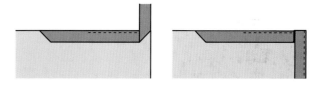

❼ Stitch from the fold of the binding along the second edge of the quilt top, stopping ¼" from the corner as before. Repeat the stitching and mitering process on the remaining edges and corners.

❽ When you reach the starting point, cut the end 1" longer than needed and tuck the end inside the beginning. Stitch the rest of the binding.

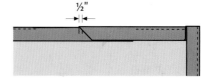

❾ Fold the binding over the raw edges of the quilt to the back and blindstitch in place.

You might enjoy these other fine titles from
MARTINGALE & COMPANY

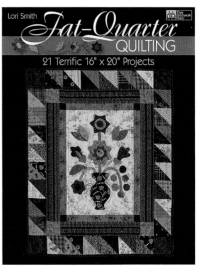

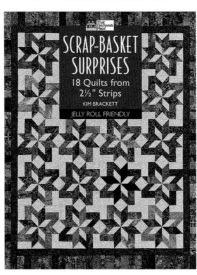

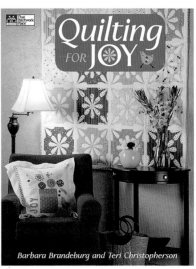

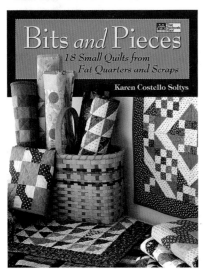

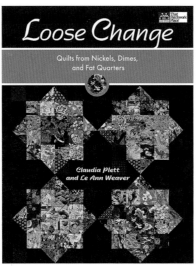

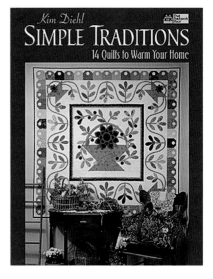

Our books are available at bookstores and your favorite craft, fabric, and yarn retailers.
Visit us at www.martingale-pub.com or contact us at:

1-800-426-3126
International: 1-425-483-3313
Fax: 1-425-486-7596
Email: Info@martingale-pub.com

Martingale®
& COMPANY

America's Best-Loved Craft & Hobby Books®
America's Best-Loved Knitting Books®

That
Patchwork
Place®

America's Best-Loved Quiting
Books®